Jehovah's Park Versus Jurassic Park

By Catie Frates
Media Angels
Ft. Myers, Florida

Jehovah's Park versus Jurrassic Park
© 2002 Catie Frates
ISBN # 1-931941-00-9
Published by Media Angels
Ft. Myers, FL 33912

www.MediaAngels.com
email MediaAngels@aol.com

Jurassic Park® is a registered trademark of Universal City Studios, Inc. and Amblin' Entertainment, Inc. This book, the author and the publisher are not associated or affiliated with, or licensed or approved by Universal City Studios, Inc. or Amblin' Entertainment, Inc.

All Scripture verses are from the King James Bible or the New American Standard Bible.

All rights reserved. No part of this publication may be produced, stored in a retrieval system or transmitted in any form by any means, electronic, mechanical, photocopy, recording or any other wire, without the prior permission of the publisher, except as provided by USA copyright law.

Cover illustration © 2002 Richard Jeffus
Illustrations ©2002 Richard Jeffus
Contact Richard Jeffus at www.VisualManna.com
email: arthis@rollanet.org

Printed in the United States of America

This book is dedicated to my dinosaur of a dad, Bill Mathews.

Acknowledgements

First and foremost, I'd like to thank God for making this project possible, for providing all the great people who have helped with this project, and for all the blessings He has showered on me and my family. Thanks to Felice Gerwitz, my friend and publisher, for following God's leading on pursuing this project, for all her encouragement and direction, diligent effort and hard work, but most of all for being the prayer warrior who constantly went to battle for us in the spiritual realm. Thanks to my editor, for her diligent and prayerful battle to help me write in understandable, proper English. Thanks to Richard Overman of Creation Educational Resources of Orange Park, FL, for his servant's heart and for kindly reading multiple manuscripts and making invaluable technical suggestions. Thanks to Rich Jeffus for his awesome illustrations, his jovial spirit under pressure, the speed with which he worked, and his desire to share the evidence for creation and the gospel. Thanks to Susan Holt, Ida Lindsey, Colleen Davidson, and Carol Platt for proof-reading and other suggestions. Thanks to the DeRosa family for all their suggestions, help, encouragement, support, prayers, and friendship. Thanks to my friend, Mike Chowman, for the extensive dinosaur resource lists he furnished. Thanks to all our other loyal friends and supporters for all their continued prayer support. Thanks to my dad and mom, Bill and Cathy Mathews for all the help, support, encouragement and for taking care of my family so very many times so that I could work in peace. Thanks to my oldest daughter and right-arm, Laina, for reading multiple manuscripts, for choosing the glossary terms, and most of all for keeping our home functioning while I was working on this project. Thanks to my beloved husband Steve, and my daughters Briesa and Kyala for living with me and still loving me through the struggles and spiritual battles of this project.

Table of Contents

Introduction 9

Chapter One - Perspectives 11
    Biblical Spectacles versus Naturalistic Spectacles 13
    Empirical Science versus Historical Science 16

Chapter Two - Scientific Interpretations 17
    Megalosaurus 20
    Iguanodon 21
    Brontosaurus 21
    Sauropod Nostril Location 22
    Dinosaurs Evolving into Birds? 23
    Warm- or Cold-Blooded 24
    Tyrannosaurus rex: Predator or Scavenger? 25

Chapter Three - The Rediscovery of Dinosaurs 29

Chapter Four - Different Dinosaurs 35
    Dinosaur Classification Chart 36
    Basic Classifications 41
    Part One - Saurischians - Lizard-Hipped 42
        Sauropods - The Gentle Giants 42
        Theropods - Upright Walking Carnivores 45
        Carnosaurs - Tyrannosaurs and Allosaurs 48
    Part Two - Ornithischians - Bird-Hipped 52
        Ceratopsids - Horned and Frilled Lizards 52
        Stegosaurs - Plated Lizards 56
        Ankylosaurs - Armored Lizards 58
        Nodosaurs - Node Lizards 59
        Ornithopods - Bird-Footed Herbivores 60
        Hadrosaurs - Duck-billed Herbivores 63
    Part Three - Pterosaurs - Winged Lizards 68
    Part Four - Sea Dragons 70

Chapter Five - Enter **Jehovah's Park** 73
    Requirements to Enter **Jehovah's Park** 75
    Dinosaurs and Dragons in the Bible 76

Chapter Six - Land Dragons and Man	83
Secular History	85
Chinese Dragons	86
Other Eastern Dragons	88
Dragons in the Epic Poem "Beowulf"	89
European and Western Dragons	90
African Dragons	96
Australian Dragons	98
Chapter Seven - Flying Dragons	99
Chapter Eight - Sea Dragons	107
Chapter Nine - Lake Dragons	117
Europe	119
Asia	123
United States of America	124
Canada	127
Australia	129
Africa	129
Chapter Ten - Dinosaurs Recorded in Art	131
Chapter Eleven - Twentieth Century Dinosaurs?!	141
Chapter Twelve - Enter **Jurassic Park**	147
The Dinosaurs' Demise	149
Translating an Evolutionary Interpretation into a Biblical Interpretation	151
Helping Others See through Biblical Spectacles	151
Conclusion	152

Appendix A - Biblical Creationism versus Naturalism
    Biblical Creationism 154
    Naturalism (Evolutionism) 155

Appendix B - The Creation Interpretation of Natural History
    Part 1 - The Recent Creation 158
    Part 2 - The Creation Week and the Fall 159
    Part 3 - "The Rains Came Down and the Flood Came Up!" 162
    Part 4 - Rocks and Fossils 164
    Part 5 - Evidence of a World-Covering Flood and Recent
             Catastrophic Deposition of Rocks and Fossils 166
    Part 6 - The Flood Waters Recede 167
    Part 7 - The Post-Flood Ice Age 169

Appendix C - The Geologic Column 171
    The Creation Interpretation of the Geologic Column 172

Appendix D - Evidence of Rapid Fossilization 177

Appendix E - Adaptation 177

Appendix F - Dangers of Old Earth Beliefs within the Church 178

Appendix G - The Gap Theory 182

Appendix H - Dinosaur Digs with Creation Expeditions 182

Endnotes 184

Glossary 187

Bibliography 189

Index 190

Elephant and Triceratops

Introduction

"Dinosaurs!" If your mind doesn't race immediately to a movie, then just hearing the word might cause your imagination to open the floral curtain of lush tropical rain forests or peer through the mist of moss-draped cypress swamps. Lurking in these beautiful and rather intimidating places are strange monsters of gargantuan size. These were once real monsters, not just the imagination of some inventive author. They were actually hatched or born, knew hunger and pain, grew and played, matured and had families. They sought food and shelter, breathed air, felt the hot summer sun and the cool evening breezes. They were fellow creatures of planet earth, yet aliens to us because they are now so foreign to our daily life.

The main purpose of this book is to introduce you to the Biblical view of dinosaurs and natural history, referred to here as Jehovah's Park. The second purpose is to briefly compare the Biblical view to the popular naturalistic/evolutionary view, referred to here as Jurassic Park. The evidence is compelling and interesting, so enjoy your journey through *Jehovah's Park versus Jurassic Park*.

Two Dragons

Chapter One

Perspectives

Biblical Spectacles versus Naturalistic Spectacles

Before we go any further, it's important to establish some ground rules. Scientific facts are interpreted, and all scientists are fallible, biased human beings. Those who believe the Bible to be the authoritative, inerrant, infallible, revealed, inspired Word of God in every area will interpret even scientific facts through that belief system. Others interpret the facts through the Naturalistic belief system. True Naturalism rules out supernatural explanations; everything must be explained by totally natural, physical means. Evolution is the naturalist's explanation for life.

It's as if scientists use special glasses through which they view the facts. The Naturalistic Spectacles give a very different picture than the Biblical Spectacles reveal, even though the facts are the same. The spectacles used to read the facts greatly alter how they are viewed, researched, and interpreted by the scientist, and how they are presented to the public.

Naturalistic Spectacles are used to view and interpret facts in most places, including many seminaries, and Christian schools and colleges. Many Christians are unaware that a scientifically valid interpretation exists using Biblical Spectacles. They believe the Bible yet view things, including their Bible, through Naturalistic Spectacles. This produces a variety of views, which fall in between strict young earth creationism, called Biblical Creationism, and Absolute Naturalistic Evolutionism. These in-between views include Old Earth Creationism, Progressive Creationism, and Theistic Evolution, which are defined in the glossary.

Most people don't realize that contradictions arise when Scripture is viewed through Naturalistic Spectacles. An example is viewing death as being a natural part of God's creation, or death existing before man sinned rather than being a direct consequence of man's sin. (For more information on this, please refer to Appendix F.) To compensate for these contradictions, the Bible usually ends up being molded to fit man's fallible, ever-changing scientific interpretations, which were made through Naturalistic Spectacles in the first place!

The perspective of this book is to look at the scientific facts through Biblical Spectacles and to expose readers to a perspective that is not "politically correct" and therefore frequently unknown. This is not meant to be offensive to those who might hold other views, but rather to broaden their awareness of this perspective and the evidence which supports it. Considering that most scientific facts will be interpreted through one of these two views, it's important to understand the conclusions and guidelines used by each. A very brief summary is given here, while a more in-depth explanation may be found in Appendix A.

Biblical Spectacles

The foundation of Biblical Creationism is accepting Genesis as a literal history, to be believed as it is written. This is the most important part of putting on (scientifically) Biblical Spectacles and leads to the following conclusions and guidelines. The earth is about 6000 years old. Living things reproduce only after their own kind (which is a broader category than species). This allows for a large number of variations within each kind (such as dogs, wolves, jackals, hyenas, etc.), but not changes to a different kind (such as fish turning into frogs or frogs turning into lizards). The original creation was perfect with no death or disease until after Adam and Eve sinned, which brought the whole creation under the curse of death, the state in which we now see it. Because of sin and the curse, devolution, not evolution, occurs. Mutation (copying errors in genetic material) causes a loss of hereditary information, not the creation of new traits and new kinds of life forms. The fossils and rocks in which they are found are relatively "young" (less than 6000 years old) and "of catastrophic origin," formed by the worldwide Flood of Noah's time and its after-effects.

Dinosaurs through Biblical Spectacles were created 6000 years ago and lived alongside man both before and after the Genesis Flood.

Biblical Spectacles

1. The earth is about 6000 years old.
2. Living things reproduce only after their own kind.
3. Death is a direct consequence of man's sin.
4. Mutation causes a loss of genetic information.
5. Devolution is occurring, not evolution.
6. The rocks and fossils are relatively young and of catastrophic origin.
7. Man and dinosaurs lived together.

Naturalistic Spectacles

A view of the universe through the Naturalist's Spectacles leads to very different conclusions. The earth is about 5,000,000,000 (5 billion) years old. Living organisms do change 'kind,' moving from lower to higher life forms (evolution, not devolution). Death and extinction have always been a part of the earth's history and help in the gradual evolutionary climb from one kind to another through natural selection and survival of the fittest. (Please realize, through Biblical Spectacles, natural selection is God's way of allowing the best-suited individuals to perpetuate their kind and pass on their beneficial genetic characteristics, which they already possess, to their offspring.) Adaptation through genetic mutation causes the appearance of new traits and eventually new kinds of life forms. The fossils and rocks in which they are found were laid down gradually over millions and billions of years.

Through the Naturalist's Spectacles, dinosaurs died off around 65 million years ago during the Cretaceous Period. People didn't evolve until about 3 million years ago, so man and dinosaurs missed meeting by over 60 million years.

Please notice that these viewpoints are diametrically opposed. There is not a good way of compromising or blending these two systems.

Naturalistic Spectacles

1. The earth is about 5 billion years old.
2. Living things change kind, leading to more complex organisms.
3. Death and extinction assist in the evolutionary climb in complexity.
4. Mutation gives rise to new traits and eventually new life forms.
5. Evolution, not devolution, is occurring.
6. The rocks and fossils are ancient and were gradually laid down.
7. Dinosaurs died off long before man evolved.

Empirical Science versus Historical Science

It is important to realize that both creation and evolution fall outside of the realm of empirical science, which involves models, hypotheses, and theories testable by observation and experimentation. No one saw God speak the universe into existence, nor has anyone ever seen change-in-kind evolution and adaptation/mutation causing an increase in genetic information. Neither event can be experimentally repeated. Creation and Evolution are historical sciences. They must be studied by investigating the effects of past events using observable evidence as clues. It is similar to forensic science; the scientist strives to determine what happened in the past from the pieces of the puzzle not yet destroyed by time. Strive as he might, he cannot be sure his conclusions are correct. Eyewitness accounts are extremely helpful in determining the truth about the past and in evaluating the observable evidence.

No eyewitness accounts of the Naturalistic history exist, so as with Biblical Creationism, scientists must place their "faith" in the scenario they choose to explain past events. The sad part is that most people don't realize we are being taught Naturalism and Evolution as if they were scientific facts, even though they're not. When we watch movies, go to museums or read books about dinosaurs, we are usually presented with the Naturalistic/Evolutionary interpretation. We are being shown the universe through the Naturalist's Spectacles, as if no other viable, logical, scientific view exists. We are so inundated with the Naturalistic perspective of dinosaurs that most Bible-believing individuals have very little, if any, idea how dinosaurs fit into their Bible. They wouldn't have a clue how to explain a Biblical view of the great reptiles to a non-Bible-believing friend or loved one.

Chapter Two

Scientific Interpretations

Scientific Interpretations

Learning about dinosaurs is a tricky business. Scientists can't just take a jaunt down to the local zoo (or any zoo, for that matter) and get blood and tissue samples from dinosaurs. Nor can they gather their backpack, tents, and other equipment to go camping in Big Cypress Swamp and observe them in their natural habitat. Fossils are the predominant empirical evidence scientists have to unveil the mystery shrouding these mighty creatures. The fossils are preserved pictures and pieces, clues frozen in time. They are found in mines, mountainsides, riverbeds, deserts, and various other places worldwide, including Antarctica.

Unfortunately, these fossils are not found with the dinosaurs' diaries, such as *The Triceratops Tribune, Jurassic Journal,* or other written records that are helpful in uncovering some of history's mysteries about the life and times of the dinosaurs. All that the fossils tell us for certain is " Hi! I'm definitely dead!"

Today's scientists find dinosaur fossils in graves that are mixed with the remains of other creatures, sometimes hundreds of them. Usually, fossil skeletons are incomplete, and most paleontologists have never seen a living dinosaur. It's like trying to reassemble thousands of tiny jigsaw puzzle pieces from several different puzzles without having all of the pieces or the benefit of seeing the box tops!

Yet frequently, the description of these creatures from their fossil remains is so complete that you would almost get the impression that someone had made eyewitness observations in order to give such specific details. How is that possible?

Paleontologists study body fossils such as bones, teeth, and claws in an attempt to determine what dinosaurs looked like, and they study trace fossils such as tracks, trails, gnaw marks, eggs, nests, gizzard stones, skin imprints, and even coprolite (a fancy word for fossil dung) to determine something of their behavior. As precious new fossil treasures are discovered, scientists reinterpret, update, refine, and sometimes discard old ideas and replace them with altogether new ones. Scientific interpretations are constantly changing as knowledge increases; however, the fossil facts remain the same. The following examples show how scientific interpretations frequently change.

1854 *Megalosaurus* interpretation versus current interpretation

Megalosaurus

The term dinosaur was first used by Richard Owen. In 1854, he made an interpretation of *Megalosaurus* (meaning "giant lizard"). As more *Megalosaurus* remains were found, scientists got a better idea of how it might have looked. Even now, we don't really know what it looked like because we are merely interpreting the fossils without direct observations.

Iguanodon

In the early 19th century, *Iguanodon* was thought to have a horn on his nose. In 1877, thirty nearly-intact *Iguanodons* were found in a Belgian mine 1000 feet below the earth's surface. The "horn" was discovered to actually be ***the animal's thumb***. OOPS!

Brontosaurus

In the late 19th century, a heated competition raged between two American paleontologists, Othniel Marsh and Edward Cope. This competition became known as the Dinosaur Bone Wars. So that Marsh could be credited for the scientific discovery of yet another new species of dinosaur in his race with Cope, the head of a *Diplodocus* from one quarry was put on the fossil body of an *Apatosaurus* from another. Thus, a new dinosaur was discovered, the ever-popular *Brontosaurus*.

Just hearing the word *Brontosaurus* brings a picture to most people's minds: a huge herbivorous dinosaur with a small head, a very long neck, and a bulky body supported on four legs like tree-trunks, all trailed by an extremely long tapering tail. As a child, I remember seeing drawings of the *Brontosaurus* walking beside three fire engines for scale in picture books. Sadly, the *Brontosaurus* never really existed. It was actually a composite of two different dinosaurs, the body of an *Apatosaurus* and the head of a *Diplodocus*.

Almost a century later, Dr. Jack McIntosh and Dr. David Berman finally convinced the scientific community that the *Brontosaurus* was really nothing more than a composite of two previously discovered long-necked, gentle giants called *Sauropods*, not a new type of dinosaur. The outcome of this controversy is that *Brontosaurus* is no longer considered a valid scientific name of an actual dinosaur.

Sauropod Nostril Location

Sauropods, such as the *Apatosaurus* and *Diplodocus*, from which the *Brontosaurus* was constructed, were estimated to have weighed 20-80 tons. Due to their great weight, 19th century paleontologists believed they spent most of their time submerged in water to support their huge bodies. This led scientists to place the nostrils at the top of the head, which seemed to be confirmed in 1884 when an intact *Diplodocus* skull was found. Scientists decided the large hole at the top of the snout must have held the entire breathing apparatus; but fossil bones alone don't reveal the location of the nostrils.

Scientist Dr. Lawrence Witmer says placement of the nostrils high on the head was "based more on history than science." Recently, Witmer compared dinosaur skulls with skulls of 62 animals. The animals chosen were from 45 species of crocodiles, birds, and lizards; all three groups are believed by evolutionists to be living relatives of dinosaurs. Witmer believes *Sauropod* nostrils were at the end of the snout, as in most reptiles today. "We found an extraordinary amount of evidence to suggest the nostrils of dinosaurs actually were parked out front," he states after closely examining fossil *Sauropod* skulls. The dinosaur picture books may have to be redrawn again![1]

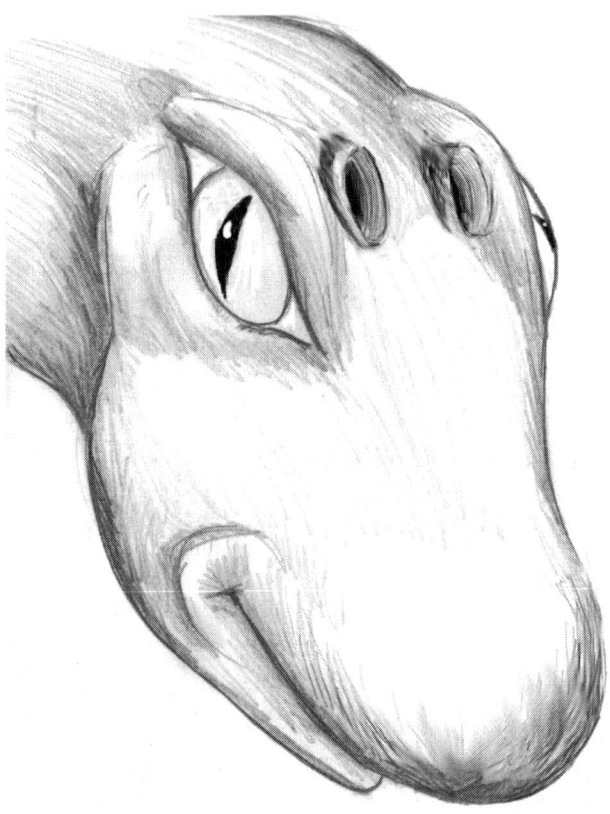

Dinosaurs Evolving into Birds?

Many current sources teach that dinosaurs aren't really gone; they are today's birds. The American Museum of Natural History in their book *Discovering Dinosaurs* classifies birds as "species of living *Theropod* dinosaurs (birds)." Did dinosaurs evolve into birds?

On a regular basis, the news media reports the discovery of the proverbial missing link between reptiles and birds composed of a small reptile fossil with feathers. Such a find would be incredible, because feathers are unique to birds. Without fail, these feathered dinosaur fossils are exaggerated, misinterpreted, or fraudulently represented.

Evolutionary biologist Alan Feduccia, who wrote *The Origin and Evolution of the Bird,* challenges the idea of dinosaurs evolving into birds in his second chapter. Feduccia points out (from his evolutionary perspective) that *Archaeopteryx* was the first real bird, with feathers, hollow bones, a wishbone, etc., and is dated as having lived 150 million years ago. If it was already a bird 150 million years ago, there were birds living at the same time as the dinosaurs, so obviously dinosaurs did not evolve into birds!

Professor John Ruben of Oregon State University stated in his book on dinosaur physiology that the similarities between certain dinosaurs and birds are purely superficial, due to the fact that they both ran a lot.

One of the largest supporters of the dinosaur-to-bird evolution idea is the American Museum of Natural History. They have spent millions of dollars renovating their exhibit showing dinosaur-to-bird evolution, though the idea is controversial at best, even within evolutionary science.

Warm- or Cold-Blooded

It is currently debated whether dinosaurs were warm- or cold-blooded. Warm-blooded animals, such as mammals and birds, regulate their body temperature by internal processes. Cold-blooded animals use outside means to regulate their body heat. Today's reptiles are cold-blooded; but from dinosaur fossils alone, there is no way to know for sure whether they were warm-blooded or cold-blooded. Many scientists hope that dinosaurs were warm-blooded like birds, because if they were, it would make their evolutionary metamorphosis from dinosaurs to birds easier to believe.

Reptiles today are cold-blooded, while mammals are warm-blooded.

Tyrannosaurus rex: Predator or Scavenger?

Another controversy surrounds a more familiar dinosaur, the gigantic-jawed, serrated-fanged, bipedal (upright walking) terror *Tyrannosaurus rex*. It is popularly portrayed by Hollywood as the biggest meanest predator that ever existed (unless, of course, you count *Jurassic Park 3*, where it was beaten by a very feisty *Spinosaurus* who ate a satellite phone). In the children's movie *Dinosaurs*, an elderly *Triceratops* described it as a "mouth full of teeth with a bad attitude." Since we cannot observe a live *T. rex*, no one really knows if it was a predator or a very large scavenger or both. *T. rex* could have served the ecosystem by cleaning up the carcasses of other huge reptiles when they died. Predator or scavenger . . . that is the question!

**SECRET TOOLS OF A T. REX
(REMOVING PREHISTORIC ROAD KILL)**

We know from the fossils that *T. rex* had very large (banana-sized) serrated teeth. Because of its dental prowess, some paleontologists picture it as a dangerous predator with basically no natural enemies (except for volcanoes or floods. Oops!). Others argue there are many herbivores with very large sharp teeth. Panda bears have big sharp dangerous teeth, and they eat bamboo predominantly. Fruit bats have big sharp teeth, and they are vegetarians. In 1917 a *T. rex* fossil was found that didn't show much dental wear. The scientists interpreted this as possible evidence that *T. rex* was a scavenger, which ate soft rotting meat, rather than a predator, which ate tough fresh flesh.

There are those who say *T. rex*'s dental roots were too shallow to sustain a predatory lifestyle, because shaking things to death and eating raw meat require strong, well-rooted teeth. Therefore, a dinosaur with weak roots might lose some of its teeth, after one good head-shaking kill; then it would have been a very hungry dinosaur. Other studies have refuted this information and tried to show evidence that *T. rex* had very strong teeth and roots. Either way, it does not help us draw a conclusion as to whether it was a predator or a scavenger.

A CAT scan was performed on a giant *T. rex* skull, the size of a Herbie-the-Love-Bug car, in an attempt to discover facts about its brain. It apparently had a small optic lobe, which was interpreted as *T. rex* having poor vision. It also had a large olfactory lobe, interpreted as it having a good sense of smell. If true, *T. rex* might have found it difficult to find prey, especially on a windy day. If it were a scavenger instead of a predator, then its poor vision wouldn't matter because dead things don't hide very well, and its good sniffer would have led it to the definitively foul odor of rotting flesh, even on a windy day.

T. rex had relatively small forelimbs, which could have presented a problem if it were

a predator. If it managed to find its prey with its poor vision and bit it and it didn't die right away, a writhing, thrashing escape attempt would have probably followed. T. rex's tiny forelimbs might have proved very inadequate to shield against the bludgeoning it could receive from its prey's life or death struggle.

Dinosaur expert Professor James Farlow of Indiana's Purdue University says if you wanted to kill a *T. rex*, all you'd have to do is trip it. Farlow and a physicist colleague have calculated that if a large *T. rex* fell while running, its tumbling torso would tear up the terrain with 6 g's of force (six times the acceleration due to gravity). Its tiny forelimbs would be of little assistance in breaking the fall. The impact of the *T. rex's* weight combined with the estimated speed of the fall would make a crater 8 inches deep in dry ground! By the time its head hit the ground, it would hit with 12 g's of force, thereby delivering a damaging, if not lethal, blow. Farlow says a fall at any speed could have been lethal for some of the larger dinosaurs.[2] The idea that God would create an animal that could die just by tripping is absolutely offensive to many people, and understandably so. I had one student suggest that the body shape resembled that of a kangaroo, and they hop around just fine; maybe *T. rex* did too. Once again, we just don't know for sure.

As to the *T. rex* debate, since we cannot observe its dining habits or running abilities, and the fossil evidence is inconclusive, we can't know if they were predators or scavengers. (There is a historical solution to this mystery, which we will explore in Chapter 6 under the section Dragons in the Epic Poem Beowulf.)

Obviously, there are many controversies surrounding dinosaurs, because interpretations are limited by the availability of evidence and the fallibility of people.

Iguanadon and Horse

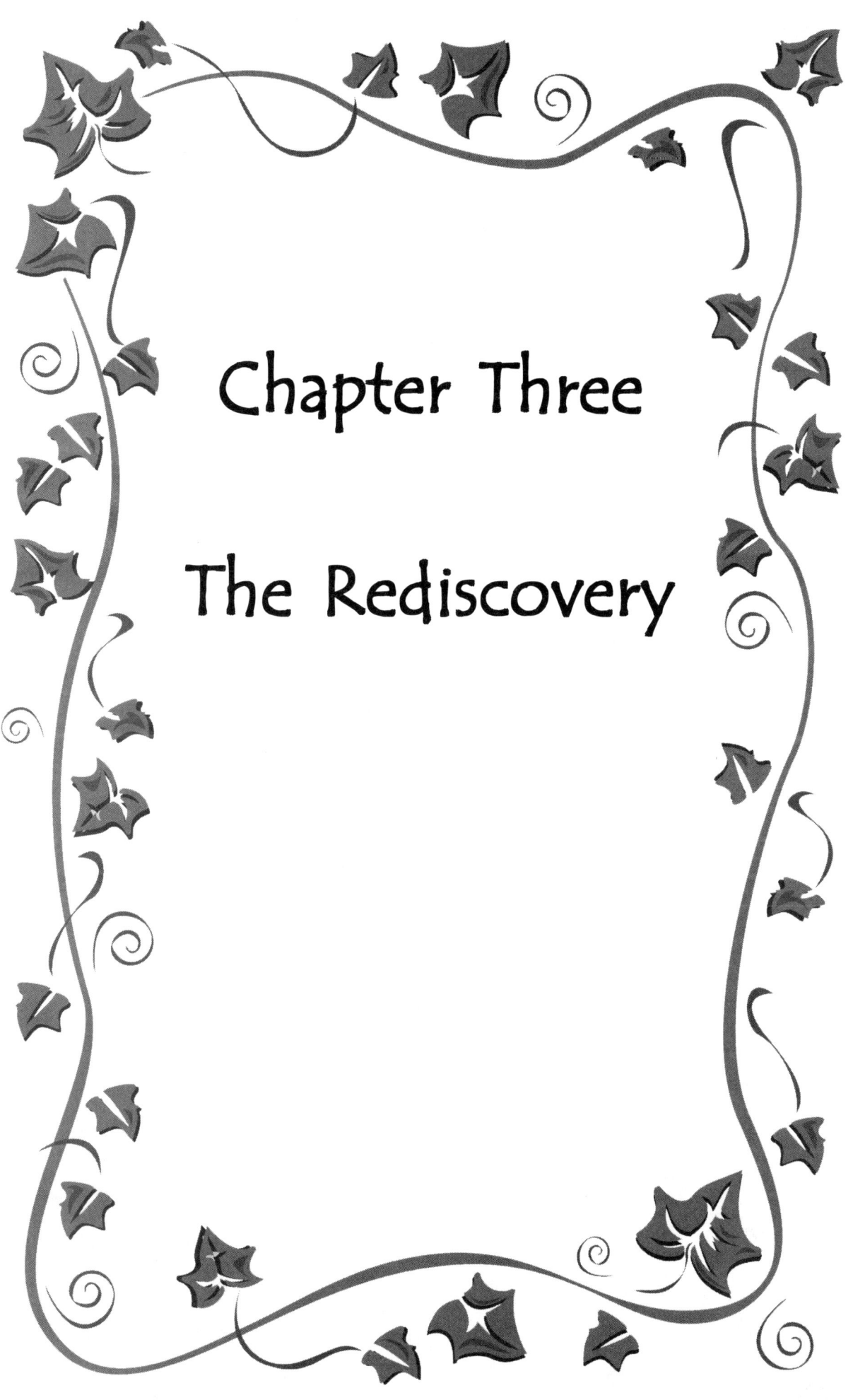

Chapter Three

The Rediscovery

The Rediscovery of Dinosaurs

Human fossil footprints alongside dinosaur footprints are evidence that man was intimately aware of dinosaurs in the past. The Paluxy River bed near Glen Rose, Texas, has many examples of human footprints and moccasin tracks in close proximity to dinosaur footprints. Over one hundred human trails, striding left to right, have been studied in this area, including tracks ranging in size from a small child to adults with foot sizes on average from 7-13. Bear, saber-toothed tiger, and mammoth tracks were found as well.[3] Human tracks with dinosaur tracks have also been reported at Kayenta Formation in Tuba City, Arizona. Native American locals have apparently been aware of their existence for a long time.[4] In 1995 Russian journalist Alexander Bushev reported the find of more than 3000 giant three-toed dinosaur footprints with bare human footprints among them in Turkmenistan.

In the early 1800's, dinosaurs were rediscovered when fossil remains of these gigantic reptiles were accidentally unearthed in mines and quarries. They sparked the curiosity of many European intellectuals. Local people identified them as dragon remains and understandably so, since they were part of their folklore that had disappeared from daily life generations earlier. While scientists disagreed about exactly what they were, eventually it became clear that they were different from contemporary reptiles, and not just in size. In 1841, Sir Richard Owen, one of England's leading anatomists, as well as a Christian and creationist, christened them "Dinosaurs," which means "fearfully great lizards" (often translated "terrible or thunder lizards").

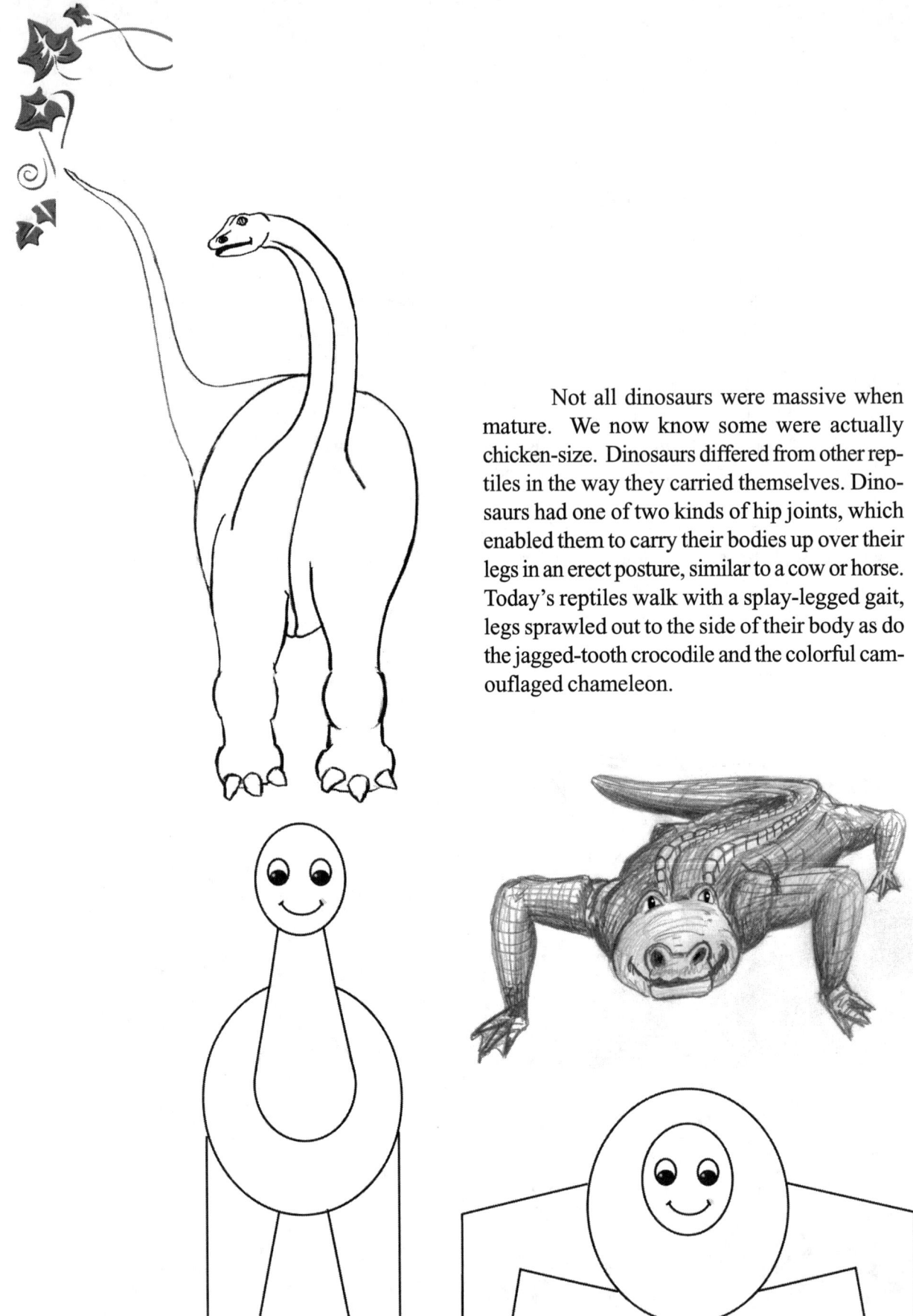

Not all dinosaurs were massive when mature. We now know some were actually chicken-size. Dinosaurs differed from other reptiles in the way they carried themselves. Dinosaurs had one of two kinds of hip joints, which enabled them to carry their bodies up over their legs in an erect posture, similar to a cow or horse. Today's reptiles walk with a splay-legged gait, legs sprawled out to the side of their body as do the jagged-tooth crocodile and the colorful camouflaged chameleon.

Some other things that researchers say most dinosaurs have in common are the following: a large hole in the bottom of their basin-shaped hip socket, a secondary palate enabling a dinosaur to eat and breath at the same time (which most reptiles cannot do), a fairly straight thigh bone of which the top turned inward, a diapsid skull which had two pairs of holes in the temporal region (crocodiles also have a diapsid skull), elbows on the front legs that pointed backwards, knees on the rear-legs pointed forward, hind legs that were larger than their forelimbs (in most instances), and they were land dwelling creatures.[5]

Even though the amazing winged and marine reptiles of the past don't fit into our dinosaur designation, most of us picture them readily when we hear the term dinosaur, probably because we've been taught for so long that they shared that steamy primordial swamp together. *Pterosaurs* were flying reptiles thought to have had glistening skin (from historic accounts). Some had razor-toothed beaks and wings which could match the wing-span of small planes. *Plesiosaurs, Kronosaurs* and *Ichthyosaurs* were believed to have been terrifying, four-finned, sharp-toothed, stealthy predators of the deep, a sailor's worst nightmare in the flesh and tooth. Our study will cover land, air, and marine reptiles, all the fearfully great lizards, not just the land reptiles we presently designate as dinosaurs.

As we take a brief look at the different types of dinosaurs, keep in mind that the fossil evidence is usually being interpreted by people who have never seen a living dinosaur. When interpretations include weights and details about their behavior and how they lived, remember that they are just interpretations and could be partially or totally incorrect, as pointed out in Chapter Two - Scientific Interpretations.

Sometimes what are described as different species of dinosaurs are really variations within kind or speciation explained further in Appendix A. Variations between males and females or older versus younger specimens may also be interpreted as different species. It is an easy and understandable mistake when it happens (remember *Brontosaurus*) and should be kept in mind as we explore the various designations.

Hadrosaurs

Chapter Four

Different Dinosaurs

Dinosaur Classification Chart

Saurischian (sore-IH-shee-an) *"Lizard-Hipped"*

   Sauropods (SORE-oh-pods)

      Apatosaurus (ah-pat-oh-SORE-us)
      Camarasaurus (kam-ar-ah-SORE-us)
      Diplodocus (dip-LOD-oh-kus)
      Brachiosaurus (brack-ee-oh-SORE-us)

   Theropods (THAIR-oh-pods)

      Coelurosaurs (seel-ur-oh-SORES)

        Compsognathus (komp-soh-NAY-thus)
        Troodon (TROH-oh-don)
        Coelophysidae (see-LOAF-ih-sih-day)
        Podokesaurus (poh-doh-kuh-SORE-us)
        Struthiomimus (strooth-ee-oh-MIME-us)
        Ornithomimus (or-nith-oh-MIME-us)
        Oviraptor (ove-ih-RAP-tor)
        Deinonychus (die-no-NIKE-us)
        Velociraptor (vel-ah-sih-RAP-tor)

Theropods (continued)

Carnosaurs (KAR-no-sores)
Tyrannosaurs (tie-RAN-oh-sores)
- Tyrannosaurus rex (tie-ran-oh-SORE-us REKS)
- Tarbosaurus (tar-bo-SORE-us)
- Albertosaurus (al-bur-toh-SORE-us)
- Daspletosaurus (das-plee-toh-SORE-us)

Allosaurs (AL-oh-sores)
- Allosaurus (al-oh-SORE-us)
- Megalosaurus (MEG-ah-loh-SORE-us)
- Deinocheirus (dine-oh-KIRE-us)
- Therizinosaurus (ther-ih-zin-oh-SORE-us)
- Spinosaurus (spine-o-SORE-us)
- Acrocanthosaurus (ak-roh-kan-thoh-SORE-us)
- Ceratosaurus (sir-ah-toh-SORE-us)

Ornithischians (or-ni-THIH-shee-ans) *Bird-Hipped*

Ceratopsids (sair-ah-TOP-sids)

Triceratops (try-SAIR-ah-tops)
Torosaurus (tor-oh-SORE-us)
Eucentrosaurus (yew-sen-troh-SORE-us)
Monoclonius (mon-oh-KLONE-ee-us)
Styracosaurus (sty-rack-oh-SORE-us)

Stegosaurs (steg-oh-SORES)

Stegosaurus (steg-oh-SORE-us)
Kentrosaurus (ken-troh-SORE-us)

Ankylosaurs (an-ky-loh-SORES)

Ankylosaurus (an-ky-loh-SORE-us)

Nodosaurs (node-oh-SORES)

Polacanthus (pole-ah-KAN-thus)
Hylaeosaurus (hy-lee-oh-SORE-us)

Ornithopods (or-NITH-oh-pods)

Iguanodon (ih-GWA-noh-don)
Camptosaurus (kamp-toh-SORE-us)
Ouranosaurus (or-an-oh-SORE-us)
Hypsilophodon (hip-sih-LOAF-oh-don)
Psittacosaurus (sih-tak-oh-SORE-us)
Pachycephalosaurus (pak-ee-sef-al-oh-SORE-us)
Hadrosaurs (had-roh-SORES)

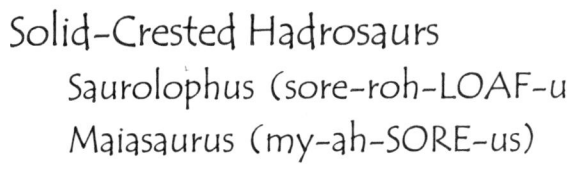

    Flat-Headed Hadrosaurs
        Edmontosaurus (ed-mont-oh-SORE-us)

Solid-Crested Hadrosaurs
    Saurolophus (sore-roh-LOAF-us)
    Maiasaurus (my-ah-SORE-us)

Hollow-Crested Hadrosaurs
    Lambeosaurs (LAM-bee-oh-sores)
        Lambeosaurus (lam-bee-oh-SORE-us)
        Corythosaurus (coh-rith-oh-SORE-us)
        Tsintaosaurus (sin-taow-SORE-us)
        Parasaurolophus (par-ah-sore-oh-LOAF-us)

Pterosaurs (tair-oh-SORES) *"Winged Lizards"*

    Rhamphorhynchus (ram-foh-RINK-us)

    Pterodactyl (tair-oh-DAK-tul)
        Pteranodon (tair-AN-oh-don)
        Quetzalcoatlus (ket-sole-koh-AT-lus)

Marine Reptiles

    Archelon (AR-kee-lon)

    Plesiosaurs (PLEE-see-oh-sores)
        Elasmosaurus (ee-LAS-moh-sore-us)

    Pliosaurs (ply-oh-SORES)
        Peloneustes (pel-oh-NEWS-tees)
        Kronosaurus (kroh-noh-SORE-us)

    Ichthyosaurs (ICK-thee-oh-sores)
        Ophthalmosaurus (op-thal-moh-SORE-us)
        Shonisaurus (show-nih-SORE-us)

Different Dinosaurs

Basic Classifications

Scientists classify living things by their similarities and differences to help them work with large amounts of information in an organized manner. Dinosaurs are presently classified in two orders. *Saurischians,* meaning "lizard-hipped," had a pelvis with 3 bones pointing in different directions and a main jawbone which held teeth; both characteristics are similar to today's reptiles. *Ornithischians,* meaning "bird-hipped," had a pelvis in which the two lower bones point backwards and a beaklike bone at the front of its jaw with teeth farther back, if at all. Neither characteristic is similar to other reptiles living today.

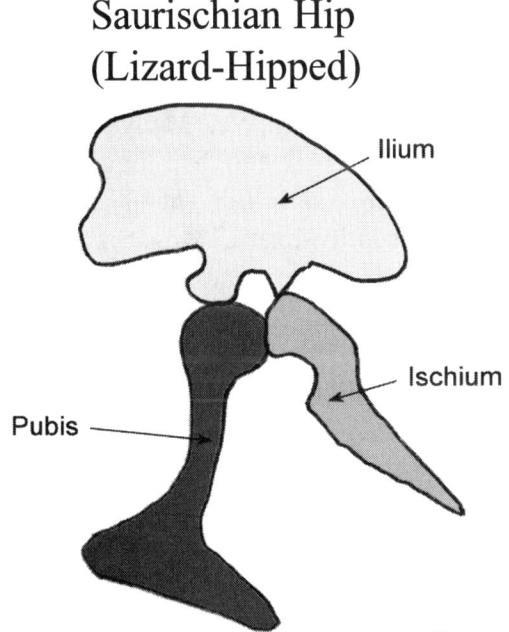

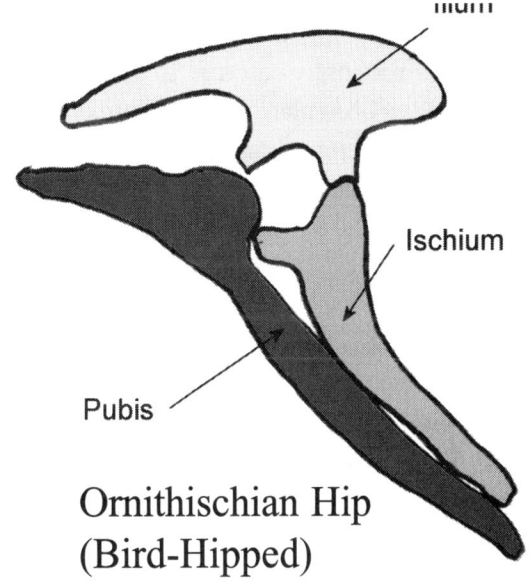

Part One

Saurischians (sore-IH-shee-ans)

Among the "lizard-hipped" *Saurischian* dinosaurs were *Sauropods,* meaning "lizard-footed," and *Theropods,* meaning "beast-footed." *Sauropods* were huge herbivorous (plant-eating) giants with long necks and tails. *Theropods* are believed to have been carnivorous dinosaurs that walked in an upright manner and acyually had bird-like (not beast-like) feet with three toes facing forward and one toe facing backward.

Sauropods (SORE-oh-pods)

The blue whale was once thought to be the largest animal God created, but since the discovery of *Sauropod* fossils in the last century, that belief appears to have been mistaken. *Sauropods* had bulky bodies, tiny heads on long slender necks, and equally long tapering tails. They are frequently referred to as "gentle giants," having been plant eaters of immense size. *Sauropods,* meaning "lizard footed," were probably named such because some of them had 5 toes like present-day lizards.

Their teeth were either pencil-like, as found in *Diplodocus,* or spoon-like, as found in *Brachiosaurus*. Either way, their teeth were in a single row and few in number. It appears their teeth were for gathering food, rather than processing, because their teeth were not sufficient in themselves to chew up the vegetation they ate. Scientists believe they swallowed jagged stones from 2 to 5 inches long called gastroliths (meaning stomach stones). They were believed to help grind up tough leaves and other plant parts, making them more digestible. Sometimes these stones are found in the stomach area of whole fossil skeletons. Two hundred gastroliths were found in one large *Diplodocus* fossil.

It is believed *Sauropods* spent the majority of their time in the water, where their body weight was supported and vegetation was plentiful and easily accessible. Many plants were within their reach, due to their long necks.

Apatosaurus (ah-pat-oh-SORE-us) means "deceptive-lizard," which is appropriate because this is the creature whose body was

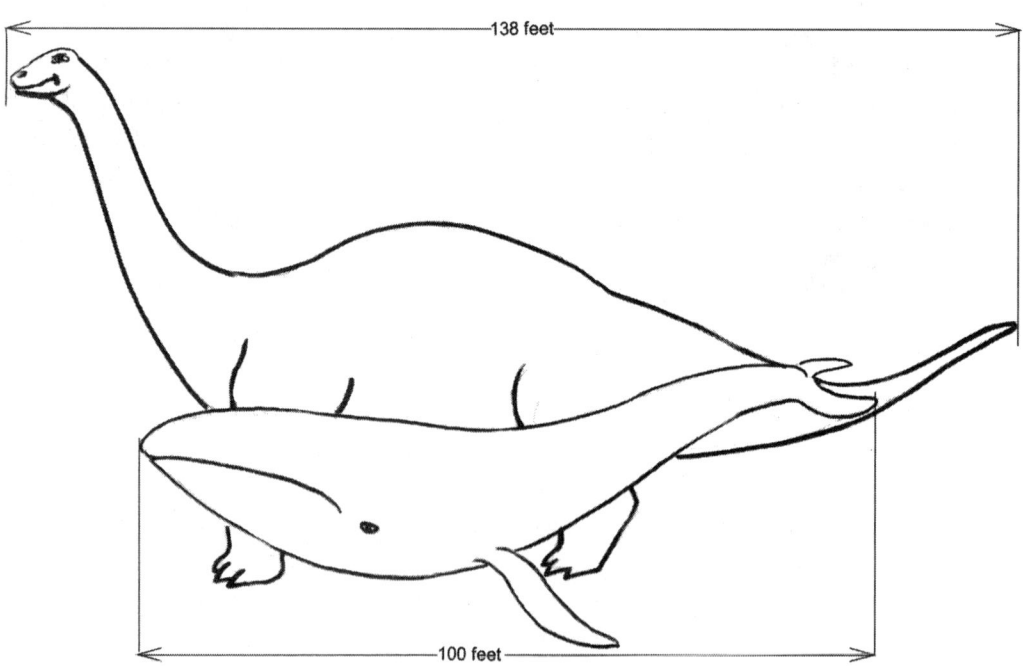

Gastroliths

used together with a *Diplodocus* head to make the *Brontosaurus* (see Chapter Two - Scientific Interpretations). *Apatosaurs* grew up to 75 feet long and are estimated to have weighed 30-40 tons. It had a small, slightly elongated head attached to a 20-foot-long neck, which contained 15 vertebrae. It stood 14 feet high at the shoulder, and its back sloped upward to a height of 17 feet at the hip, so its topline (the line from the shoulders to the hips) sloped upward from the front to the rear of the animal. Twenty-three sets of fossil tracks, with footprints 39 inches in diameter, were found in Texas. They are believed to be tracks of *Apatosaurs* or a similar species. There is no sign of tail dragging in these footprints, so it appears it held its tail up in the air.

Camarasaurus (kam-ar-ah-SORE-us) is a *Sauropod* that was about 60 feet long and is estimated to have weighed about 20 tons. Because its front legs were about 4/5 as big as the hind legs, its topline was almost horizontal. Though it had the characteristic long neck and tail of the *Sauropods*, they were much shorter than those of the *Apatosaur* or *Diplodocus*. The *Apatosaur's* teeth were loose fitting and peg-like, not designed for tougher vegetation. The *Camarasaur's* teeth were longer, sharper, and closer together, possibly enabling it to eat a wider variety of plants. These teeth were fixed in a shorter, broader-shaped head than the *Apatosaur* or *Diplodocus*.

A baby *Camarasaurus* was found in Utah. It had a heavy body, large head, and a short neck and tail. Finding juvenile dinosaurs is very helpful because it sheds light on their development.

Diplodocus (dip-LOD-oh-kus), meaning "double beams," had a very long neck and tail. Of its total 88 feet of length, it had a 26-foot neck, 16-foot body, and 46-foot tail. It was as tall as a three story building and as long as the width of a football field! Even though it was extremely long, it was believed to be only 1/3 the weight of the *Apatosaur,* making it a very slender creature. It appears God chose to design this reptile with a small brain in its skull and another type of brain receptor in the spinal column at the rear of the monster because of its great length. It had strong, heavily-built legs to support its weight, and a few of its toes were clawed. Its head was slightly elongated, almost horse-shaped in some specimens, such as the *Apatosaur*. Scientists believe *Diplodocus* was able to stand up on its hind legs from the water, plant its front legs on the bank, and extend its neck to reach its choice of vegetation.

The **Brachiosaurus** (brack-ee-oh-SORE-us) was named "arm-lizard" because it had longer forelegs than rear. Its small dome-shaped head had a broad nose and spoon-shaped teeth, attached to what scientists believe to have been weak jaws. Its shoulders at 16-19 feet tall were much higher than its hips. Its topline sloping downward to its tail had the opposite back slant of the *Apatosaurus*. It was also much larger than *Apatosaur,* weighing in around 80 tons; that's as much as twelve elephants. It was approximately 75 feet long and held its head 42 feet high, which is high enough to look in a four-story window!

Some extremely large *Sauropod* fossils have been found. The *Ultrasaurus* at 100 feet long, *Supersaurus* at 110 feet long, and *Seismosaurus* at 140 feet long were absolutely gargantuan. They are all now believed to be variations within the *Diplodocus* or *Brachiosaurus* kind (kind in the Biblical sense).

Camarasaurus, Brachiosaurus, Apatosaurus

Coelophysis

Theropods (THAIR-oh-pods)

Along with the gentle giants, order *Saurischia* includes *Theropods,* meaning "beast-footed." They were carnivorous bipeds (walked upright on two feet) with bird-like (not beast-like) feet: three toes facing forward, and one toe facing backward. *Theropods* are divided into the smaller *Coelurosauria*, meaning "hollow lizard," which includes the chicken- to ostrich-sized creatures, and the larger *Carnosaurs,* meaning "flesh-eating lizards."

Coelurosaurs (seel-ur-oh-SORES)

Compsognathus (komp-soh-NAY-thus), meaning "pretty jawed," was the smallest lightweight predator found, weighing only 7-10 pounds, making it chicken- to cat-sized and up to 3 feet long. Its skull was only 2.5 inches long with small sharp teeth. It had short forelimbs with two bird-like claws, possibly used for reaching and grasping. In this way it was very similar to *Tyrannosaurus rex*. All of the other *Coelurosaurs* had three or four fingers on their forelimbs. *Compsognathus* had long slender legs and are believed to have been good runners. In Germany, a fossil of one was found with a lizard in its stomach, suggesting lizards were part of its diet. Obviously this creature was buried very rapidly; otherwise the contents of its stomach would have been long gone by the time it became petrified.

Troodon (TROH-oh-don), meaning "wounding teeth," was named for its strange teeth, which were flat on two sides with curved, serrated edges in front and back and secured into a very thin jawbone. It was smaller than the *Oviraptor* and larger than *Podokesaurus*. It was called the cheetah of the dinosaur world because it appears to have been designed to run very quickly.

As fast as *Troodon* is believed to have been, the family **Coelophysidae** (see-LOAF-ih-sih-day), meaning "hollow nature," is believed to have been even faster, being called the swiftest in the dinosaur world. *Podokesaurus* (poh-doh-kuh-SORE-us), meaning "swift-footed lizard," was only about 2-3 feet high and 5-8 feet long with a long flexible neck and long thin tail used for balance as it ran. Because some of its bones were hollow, it is estimated to have weighed only 60 pounds. Its forelimbs were half the size of its hind legs. Some *Coelophysis* had strong knife-like teeth. One fossil was found with a small *Coelophysis* in its stomach cavity, so many believe it was both carnivorous and cannibalistic.

Struthiomimus (strooth-ee-oh-MIME-us), meaning "ostrich mimic," had hollow bones like a bird, probably to make its body lighter to run faster. Scientists believe it could run up to 45 miles per hour (as fast as the fastest racehorse in the world) with 15-foot strides. Its speed was its only apparent means of defense! It was 13 feet long from its beak to the end of its long tail, which is believed to have been used for balance when running. It was 6-8 feet tall with long slim powerful legs. Its strong slender forelimbs were equipped with long claws. Out of its short body extended a long slender neck, topped with a small head ending in a beak with no teeth, so it was unable to chew. *Ornithomimus* (or-nith-oh-MIME-us), meaning "bird mimic," was slimmer and lighter weight than *Struthiomimus*.

Oviraptor (ove-ih-RAP-tor), meaning "egg thief," was named for the first find in the Gobi Desert in Mongolia, back in 1922. The bones of this 6-foot-long *Theropod* were found with a nest of large dinosaur eggs. The skull of its small head, which is believed to have housed a large brain for a dinosaur, was crushed in the nest. Because of the way the fossil was found, scientists thought the *Oviraptor* must have been killed while trying to steal eggs, so they named it "egg thief." It could have just been deposited with the eggs by chance during the Flood; we just don't know because we've never seen one alive. It had a sharp toothless beak with two spikes that protruded from the roof of its mouth, possibly to crush small bones or eggs.

Deinonychus (die-no-NIKE-us) and *Velociraptor* (vel-ah-sih-RAP-tor) were in the family *Dromaeosaur*, meaning "running lizard." They were believed to have been extremely agile. The end of each forelimb was equipped with three sharp curved claws believed for holding prey. Its hind legs had one small toe pointed backward, with 3 toes pointed forward. The two outside toes were strong enough for supporting weight and running. The middle toe held a terrible sickle-shaped "switchblade" claw believed to be used for slashing at prey and cutting up meat. Scientists have found bony rods or stiff tendons which extended from the tailbone down the length of the tail, which held it rigid to assist in balance when running. Its remains are found in groups, so it is possible they lived or hunted in packs.

Deinonychus, meaning "bold claw," had a strong body, powerful jawbones, and blade-like teeth. It was 10-12 feet long, 3-5 feet high, and is estimated to have weighed 150-175 pounds. Its forelimbs had wrist joints, allowing it to use its wrists like we do. Some scientists believe it would balance on its tail and one leg while it cut its dinner with the slashing claw on the other hind foot. Its slashing claw on its second toe was 5 inches long! Scientists believe it was retractable and was held off the ground when the creature ran. It had three holes in its skull that helped keep it lightweight, 70 sharp serrated teeth slanting backward, a large brain, and large eyes. Many nocturnal animals have large eyes, so maybe it was a night dweller.

Velociraptor

Velociraptor, meaning "swift thief," had all the features of *Deinonychus,* only smaller. Its head and snout were low, flat, and narrow with 30 curved teeth. It stood 5 feet tall, was 6 feet long, and weighed 150 pounds. Unusual to dinosaurs, it had collarbones, which gave its forelimbs added strength.

The fossil of one *Velociraptor* was found in Mongolia, clinging to the fossil skull of a *Protoceratops*, a member of the horn-faced (*Ceratopsid)* family without a horn but with the flared collar shield and parrot beak. The *Protoceratops* skull was in the *Velociraptor's* chest, and the *Velociraptor's* claws appear to be holding the neck shield of the *Protoceratops.* Many interpret this as a death battle between them. Another explanation is that while the two reptiles were being washed away in torrential flood waters, the *Velociraptor* grabbed the passing *Protoceratops* as it floated or swam within reach, as a drowning person claws and grabs for anything floating nearby.

Carnosaurs (KAR-noh-sores)

The largest *Theropods* were the *Carnosaurs*, including the *Tyrannosaurs* and the *Allosaurs*. Both groups were large bipeds equipped with large sharp teeth and much smaller forelimbs than hind. They moved on feet with three clawed toes pointing forward and a dewclaw pointing back. One of the main differences between the two families is that the *Tyrannosaurs* had very small forelimbs ending in two claws, while *Allosaurs* had larger stronger forelimbs (half as long as their hind legs) with three fingers. Both had a jaw that hinged at the back like a snake, allowing it to open its mouth very wide, taking in large amounts of food with each bite. Like other bipedal dinosaurs, they had pivotal hip joints allowing them to rear up or bend down as needed.

Tyrannosaurs (tie-RAN-oh-sores)

Tyrannosaurus rex (tie-ran-oh-SORE-us REKS), meaning "king of the tyrant lizards," is the most famous *Theropod,* as well as the largest *Carnosaur* at 20 feet tall and 50 feet long, as long as an 18-wheeler! It is estimated to have weighed up to 7 tons. Its skull was 6 feet long with jaws opening 4 feet wide laden with 3-7 inch serrated teeth. In this huge skull was a very small brain. Its tiny forelimbs ended in two claws, as did all the *Tyrannosaurs*. Scientists speculate whether it hunted individually or in packs. Either way, it's not the kind of reptile I'd want to meet accidentally!

Tarbosaurus (tar-bo-SORE-us) was *Tyrannosaurus rex's* Asian counterpart. A Russian expedition in Mongolia in the 1940's found 7 of them. Six more were found in the 1960's by a Polish-Mongolian expedition. They were 33-46 feet long and slightly lighter-built than *T. rex,* but otherwise quite similar, with the large jaws and teeth and tiny two-clawed forelimbs. *Tarbosaurus* might have been a variation of *T. rex* or just a younger specimen than the larger heavier fossil finds. Scientists do put them in the same genus.

Albertosaurus (al-ber-toh-SORE-us) was first called *Gorgosaurus* until it was found to be the fossil of a juvenile. *Albertosaurs* have been found in Alberta, Canada, and Montana, USA. They were 20-26 feet long with a slender torso and are estimated to have weighed 2-3 tons. They were very similar to *T. rex* but had a lighter skull, longer snout, and smaller teeth, possibly a variation in the *T. rex* kind.

Daspletosaurus (das-plee-toh-SORE-us), meaning "frightful lizard," was slightly heavier than *Albertosaurus* with slightly larger forelimbs than other *Tyrannosaurs*. It could have been the fossil remains of older individuals than the *T. rex* and *Albertosaur* specimens. *Daspletosaurus* fossils were found buried with *Albertosaurus*, and with horned and duck-billed dinosaur fossils.

Tyrannosaurus

Allosaurs (AL-oh-sores)

Allosaurs were *Carnosaurs* with forelimbs much larger than those of the *Tyrannosaurs*. Each forelimb was equipped with three claws. Its hind legs were twice as long as its forelimbs, which ended in three-clawed toes.

Allosaurus (al-oh-SORE-us) was 35-40 feet long, stood 16 feet high, was 8 feet high at the hip, and is estimated to have weighed 1-3 tons. It was believed to use its long tail for balance. Its 3-foot-long head was decorated with bumps and ridges, and housed forty 4½-inch-long blade-sharp teeth on the top row and 32 on the bottom. These bottom teeth curved inward to help direct meat into its mouth. It had large eyes, twice as large as *T. rex*, meaning it either had very good vision or was nocturnal. More than forty fossil *Allosaurs* were found in Utah in 1940, so they may have lived and hunted in packs.

In October 1995, a fossil clutch of *Theropod* eggs was found in a seaside cliff in Lisbon, Portugal. Thirty-four eggs were found, one crushed open before or during fossilization. Paleontologists could see the embryo inside and even fragments of vertebrae attached to the inside of the eggshell. The *Theropod* embryo would have been 10 inches long if it had hatched, and it resembled an *Allosaur*. Surprisingly, there were three types of dinosaur eggs in the clutch, leading scientists to believe the area was a nursery site for different species of dinosaurs.[6]

Megalosaurus (meg-ah-loh-SORE-us), meaning "giant lizard," was the second dinosaur found in modern times (since the 1800's). It was 30 feet long and is believed to have been slow-moving. Its short, thick neck held a one-foot-long head equipped with large eyes and large, sharp serrated teeth. Its tail was short compared to many of the *Theropods* and was flat on two sides.

Deinocheirus (dine-oh-KIRE-us) was the size of *T. rex* equipped with 8-foot-long forelimbs ending in three fingers with 10-inch claws, thus the name *Deinocheirus*, meaning "terrible hand"! Similar 8-foot-long fossil forelimbs were found with 2-foot-long claws and were named ***Therizinosaurus*** (ther-ih-zin-no-SORE-us). It could prove to be an older *Deinocheirus* specimen.

Spinosaurus (spine-oh-SORE-us), meaning "thorn lizard," was an *Allosaur* decorated with a fin or sail on its back. Found in Egypt and Morocco, they were 40 feet long and are estimated to have weighed 7 tons. Its vertebral spines that formed the fin were up to 6 feet long. Some believe the fins were used in heat exchange to help *Spinosaurus* regulate body temperature, assuming they were cold-blooded. Unlike the other *Carnosaurs*, its teeth were straight, not curved.

Acrocanthosaurus (ak-roh-kan-thoh-SORE-us), an *Allosaur* fossil found in Oklahoma, had a long rudder-like fin or sail 14-16 inches in height, much smaller than those found on *Spinosaurus*. These creatures apparently lived in the Americas after the Flood as evidenced by South American pre-Columbian stone-art found in the Nasca Desert depicting them.

The most unique *Carnosaur* was the ***Ceratosaurus*** (sir-ah-toh-SORE-us), an *Allosaur* with a horn on its head! It was 20 feet long and similar to the *Allosaur*, but smaller. Their remains have been found in North America in a quarry with other *Allosaurs*. It had a hard head, long sharp teeth, a short thick neck, and a long heavy tail. Its hind legs had three claws, one on each toe, and its shorter forelimbs had four fingers on each hand.

Allosaur

Part Two

Ornithischians (or-ni-THIH-shee-ans)

Those creatures in the order **Ornithischia,** meaning "bird-hipped," had a pelvis in which the two lower bones (the pubis and the ischium) parallel each other and point backwards, unlike other reptiles. (*Saurischians'* 3 hipbones pointed in different directions, similar to other reptiles.) All *Ornithischians* were herbivores (plant-eaters) with a beak-like bone at the front of the jawbone, uncharacteristic of other reptiles, and teeth at the back of the jawbone, if at all.

There were five types of the "bird-hipped" *Ornithischian* dinosaurs: the *Ceratopsids,* which were horn-faced dinosaurs; the *Stegosaurs,* which had heavy bony plates, and sharp spines down their backbones; the lesser-known *Ankylosaurs* and *Nodosaurs*, which were heavily-armored, slow moving creatures; and the *Ornithopods*, which were beaked and duck-billed dinosaurs with bird-like hind feet, three toes pointing forward and one pointing back.

Ceratopsids (sair-ah-TOP-sids)

The *Ceratopsids,* meaning "horned faces," were the rhinoceros of the reptile world. Fossil remains have been found only in North America. They had short necks which held very large heavy heads decorated with horns and framed by frills of various shapes and sizes around their necks and the back of their heads and necks. Most of the short-frilled *Ceratopsids* had at least one "window," a skin-covered hollow section that reduced the weight of the heavy bony frills. Their heads ended in a parrot-like beak. Behind this beak were sharp cheek teeth on powerful jaws fastened to the frill bone.

Different *Ceratopsids* are identified today by the different horn configurations and frill shapes, although some scientists believe the differences in size and the more ornamental frills were the male of the species. If true, there weren't as many different *Ceratopsids* as believed, but just differences in the sexes. Their bodies ranged from 6 to 30 feet in length supported on short thick legs ending in four strong toes with hoof-like toenails, which were splayed out for better surface area. God designed these tank-like creatures with trellis-like bones in the hips for strength to bear their incredible weight. Their neck and shoulder regions were also strengthened. To help support their extremely heavy skulls, their first few vertebrae were fused together, and the main bones of the shoulders were securely joined.

Triceratops (try-SAIR-ah-tops), meaning "three horns," was the largest *Ceratopsid* and is many people's favorite dinosaur. It grew to 30 feet long, stood 9½ feet tall, and weighed 6 tons. There was no 'window' in its 7-foot-long skull decorated with one nose horn and up to 40-inch-long eyebrow horns curving forward, probably used for defense. Plants were chopped with its sharp beak and chewed by its sharp molars, held fast in strong jaws. Its fossils were first found in 1888 on a ranch in Wyoming. Usually found in groups, *Triceratops* are believed to have lived in herds; at least we're sure they were buried in herds.

The next biggest *Ceratopsid* is *Torosaurus* (tor-oh-SORE-us), meaning "bull lizard," named for its vicious-looking horns. It had 2-foot-long eyebrow horns framed by a huge frill with smooth edges and a horn on the end of its nose. Its skull was 8½ feet long from beak to frill-tip, the largest skull of any land animal. It was slightly shorter than *Triceratops* at 26 feet long, but was estimated to weigh 8-9 tons, actually heavier than the larger *Triceratops*.

Eucentrosaurus (yew-sen-troh-SORE-us), meaning "well-horned lizard," was previously called *Centrosaurus*. A large fossil herd of them was found buried in Canada. One paleontologist's report stated that the bones of the herd were broken and trampled as if they were stampeding while trying to cross a river. Is it possible the herd was trying to escape the torrential Flood waters when they were buried? *Eucentrosaurus* was a mid-sized *Ceratopsid* at 20 feet long. Its head had one long nose horn, while the edges of its short frill were decorated with small horn-like studs. From the top of the frill, two large spikes curved forward over the 2 frill "windows."

Monoclonius (mon-oh-KLONE-ee-us), meaning "one horn," as its name indicates, had only one long pointed nose horn. On its 6-foot-long head, it had a short frill decorated with small bony knobs. It was also a mid-sized *Ceratopsid* at 18-20 feet long.

Styracosaurus (sty-rack-oh-SORE-us), meaning "spiked lizard," was named for the spikes on the back of its frill. It had one long nose horn that stood two feet high and 6 inches thick. It was 18 feet long, stood six feet tall, and is estimated to have weighed 3-4 tons. Fossil findings led scientists to believe they cared for their young until they were full-grown.

Torosaurus

Torosaurus   *Eucentrosaurus*   *Rhino*

Monoclonius   *Triceratops*

Stegosaurs (STEG-oh-sores)

The second type of "bird-hipped" dinosaurs are the *Stegosaurs,* the plated dinosaurs. The **Stegosaurus** (steg-oh-SORE-us), was the largest representative of the plated lizards. It was found first in North America, but others have since been found in other places. Scientists originally thought the plates lay on the animals' back for protection like roof tiles and thus the name *Stegosaurus,* meaning "roofed lizard." From further fossil finds, it is now believed that the plates stood up along the back and were embedded in thick skin, not the spine. These plates, which were up to 30 inches high and 30 inches wide, were lined up in rows from just behind the head along the back and tail. The tail was equipped with two pair of spikes, rather than plates. These tail spikes were up to 3 feet long on either side, which were

probably a very formidable defense againtst creatures attacking from the rear or sides.

The fossil plates were finely grooved and honeycombed with space suggesting they had many blood vessels and circulation that ran through them. If this is true, it is further speculated that these plates were used to help regulate body temperature.

Stegosaurus was up to 30 feet long, and 8-11 feet high at the hip, which was the highest part of its body, because its hind legs were twice as long as its forelegs. Although it was a quadruped (walked down on all fours), it is believed that they could rear up on their hind legs for short periods to reach for vegetation above ground level. It is believed to be slow moving, because its long thighbone was not designed for running.

Its small, narrow, almost horse-shaped head was near the ground due to its short front legs. It was equipped with a beak, small cheek teeth, and a walnut sized brain. Just imagine, a 4000-pound body controlled by a 2½-ounce brain! Othniel Marsh made a cast of the creature's brain from a well-preserved fossil skull and was first to discover its tiny brain.

Because this was one of the first dinosaurs found and studied in the USA, scientists started to think all dinosaurs had tiny brains and were not intelligent. It is now known that *Stegosaurs* had the smallest brain of the large dinosaurs; some had much larger brain capacities.

To help compensate for this small brain capacity and give it faster reflexes in its rear end, it is believed to have been equipped with a nerve center in a space found in the tailbone about 20 feet from its brain. If this were the case, it would have provided faster reflexes in the rear end of the animal than if the nerve impulse had to travel 20 feet to the brain and 20 feet back to the area needed to respond.

Another plated dinosaur was the ***Kentrosaurus*** (ken-troh-SORE-us), meaning "spiked lizard," named for its appearance. It had plates from behind its head to the middle of its back and then almost spike-shaped, cone-like projections from the middle of its back to its tail. It is also believed to have had a pair of spikes that projected out from its thighs. Smaller than *Stegosaurus* and ranging from 8 to 16 feet long, *Kentrosaurus* was found first by a German expedition to Tanzania, Africa, in the same vicinity with *Brachiosaurs*. Either they lived in the same area with *Brachiosaurs*, or they just happened to be buried near them.

Chinese *Stegosaurs* are the ***Huayangosaurus, Tuojiangosaurus*** and ***Wuerhosaurus.*** *Tuojiangosaurus*, named for the place in China where it was discovered, was the largest of the Chinese *Stegosaurs* at 23 feet long, considerably smaller than the American *Stegosaurus*. It had two rows of triangular spike-like plates from its neck to its tail, 15 pairs in all, not including its four tail-spikes, and two shoulder-spikes. The creature did have the characteristic elongated head and spoon-shaped teeth.

Huayangosaurus was like a small 13-foot-long *Stegosaur,* but it had front and back teeth and hip spikes, unlike the *Stegosaurus*. Its plates were also slightly narrower and more pointed than its American cousin.

Ankylosaurs
(an-KY-loh-sores)

Another type of "bird-hipped" dinosaur was the armored lizard, the *Ankylosaur*, meaning "stiff lizard," the Sherman tank of the dinosaur world. Bony armor covered its back as it moved slowly on all fours almost like a cross between an armadillo and a tortoise. Its hind legs were longer than its front legs, so it moved with its relatively small head close to the ground, as did the *Stegosaurus*. Scientists believe it tore plants with its beaked mouth and then chewed with its weak cheek teeth.

Ankylosaurus (an-ky-loh-SORE-us) was 24 feet long, 4 feet high, 6 feet wide, and is estimated to have weighed 2-4 tons. Its armor must have been a fairly effective defense, because some *Ankylosaurs* reached 30 feet in length, even though they moved fairly slowly on short stumpy legs and hoofed toes. Paleontologists believe it resembled a huge armadillo in shape with bony points all over it. Its 2-foot-long triangular head was decorated with bony projections located behind the eyes. It had the characteristic *Ornithischian* beak. Its armor was curved bony plates fitted together closely in its tough leathery skin, which covered its head, neck, back, tail and even its eyelids. Along its sides was a row of sharp spikes, and at the end of its short thick tail was a strong club-like mass of bone.

Ankylosaurus

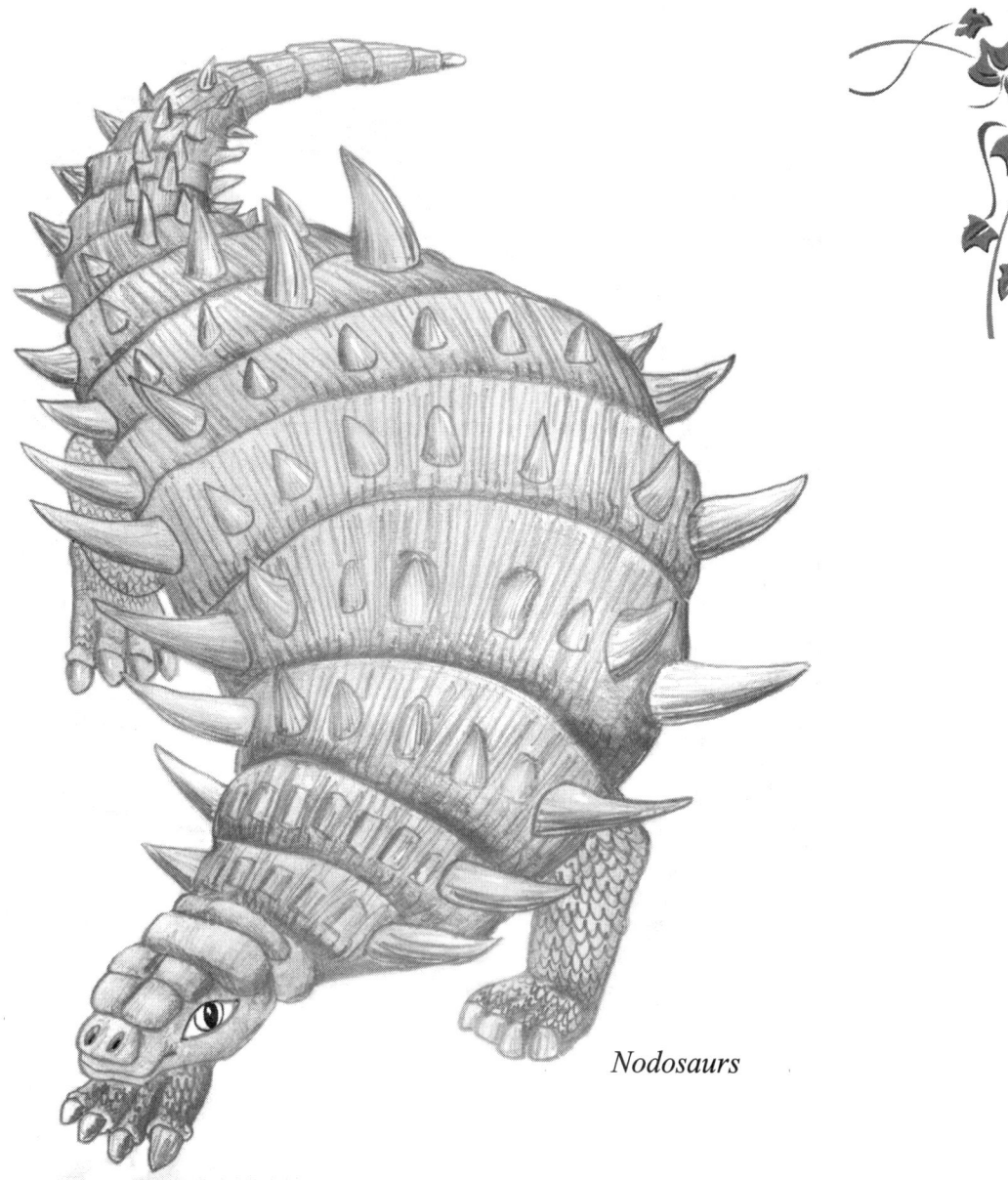

Nodosaurs

Nodosaurs
(NODE-oh-sores)

Nodosaurs, meaning "node lizards," were armored lizards, smaller than the *Ankylosaurs* and not equipped with tail-clubs. **Polacanthus** (pole-ah-KAN-thus) was a *Nodosaur* that appears to have been 13-18 feet long and 6 feet tall at the hip. The only fossil skeleton to date was discovered in England but included only the back and tail sections. It had pairs of long spines or thorn-like plates out of each side of its armor down its back and tail, and it is assumed that this pattern continued up to the neck. It appeared to be impervious to attack except possibly on its unprotected underside, similar to the *Ankylosaurs*.

Hylaeosaurus (hy-lee-oh-SORE-us), meaning "woodland lizard," was named for the forested area in the Sussex region of England where the fossil was discovered in 1833. It appears to have been around 13 feet long. Its armor had bony spikes protruding from its sides like the *Polacanthus*. Only the front half of this skeleton has been studied, because it has not been removed from its limestone tomb. Recent fossil finds indicate that its spines were in two rows standing up on the reptile's back rather than sticking out the sides as it was originally thought. Some think possibly *Polacanthus* and *Hylaeosaurus* were really the same species.

Ornithopods
(or-NITH-oh-pods)

Ornithopoda, meaning "bird-footed," were dinosaurs with three toes pointing forward and one pointing back on their hind feet. It includes a variety of beaked and duck-billed herbivores; some walked upright, some on all-fours, and some are believed to have moved both ways.

Iguanodon (i-GWA-noh-don), is historically known as one of the first dinosaurs to be described in modern times. One spring day in 1822, Mary Mantell accompanied her husband, Dr. Gideon Mantell, on a house call in England. While waiting for him, she took a walk and found a large tooth in a rock pile and showed it to her husband. Dr. Mantel realized it was unlike anything he had ever seen before; he went back to look for more teeth in the same rock pile. After conferring with many experts of the day, he finally concluded the tooth was similar to an iguana's and named the creature *Iguanodon,* meaning "iguana tooth."

We now believe *Iguanodon* was 15-33 feet long, 16 feet tall, and was a great and ponderous creature estimated to have weighed 5 tons. Its hind legs were 70% longer than its front legs with typical *Ornithopod* hind feet (three toes pointing forward and one small toe pointing back). Its front feet were equipped with four fingers and a spike-thumb possibly used for ripping vegetation. From the deep impressions of its 34-inch-long fossil footprints, paleontologists have surmised things about its stride and gait. *Iguanodon* is believed to have walked either upright or on all fours and had a muscular tail to assist it in balance. Its iguana-like teeth were located behind the typical *Ornithischian* beak.

Camptosaurus (kamp-toh-SORE-us), meaning "bent lizard," was similar to *Iguanodon*, but it was smaller (23 feet long) and lighter (a half-ton), and its femur was more curved. Its strong hind legs, which ended in four hoofed toes, were twice as long as its front legs. Though shorter, the front legs were stout and strong with 4 fingers and a spike-thumb similar to *Iguanodon*. Scientists believe it walked on all fours and had jaws with pouches (similar to squirrels) behind its beaked mouth.

Ouranosaurus (or-an-oh-SORE-us) was similar to *Camptosaurus*, but was adorned with a fin or sail like *Acrocanthosaurus*, possibly used for body temperature regulation. It had a long flat head ending in a toothless beak and was equipped with teeth back in its cheek. *Camptosaurus* and *Ouranosaurus* might have been variations within kind.

Iguanodon

Hypsilophodon (hip-sih-LOAF-oh-don), meaning "high-ridged tooth," was a rather small fleet-footed dinosaur discovered in England in 1849. It was 7½ feet long and about 2 feet high at the hip with limbs proportioned like today's fastest runners. As in gazelles, the elongated leg bones were very strong with thick upper leg bones. The five fingers on its forelimbs are believed to have been used for grasping, not climbing, and it had 4 toes on its hind feet. It had a long cord-like tail, probably used for a counter-balance when it slanted its body while running. It had a toothless beak, but its cheeks were equipped with sharp chopping teeth. In the 1980's, paleontologists in Montana found new varieties of *Hypsilophodon* in the vicinity with fossil clams, snails, algae, and a large *Pterosaur*. Thus many *Hypsilophodon* may have lived in or near an aquatic environment. At least we know they were buried in one.

Spiral-shaped clutches of dinosaur eggs were found on Egg Mountain, Montana. Dr. Jack Horner unearthed 12 separate clutches, along with juvenile *Hypsilophodons,* on 3 separate horizons, or layers of rock, one on top of another. The eggs were arranged in a spiral pattern in nests approximately 8-10 feet apart, just longer than the adult body length. From these findings, it appears these reptiles nested in colonies.

The first fossils of **Psittacosaurus** (sih-tak-oh-SORE-us), meaning "parrot lizard," named for the parrot-like beak on its face, were found in Mongolia. It was a smaller dinosaur at 6½ feet long and an estimated 50 pounds. The fossils suggest that it walked upright with its hind legs twice as long as its front legs. It had small cheek horns, and behind its parrot-like beak, it displayed well-worn teeth. Even the remains of a 10-inch-long juvenile *Psittacosaurus* had worn teeth, showing it fended for itself from a very early age. Juvenile specimens have been found. One very small individual had a 1-inch-long skull.

A particularly strange bird-hipped dinosaur was the **Pachycephalosaurus** (pak-ee-sef-al-oh-SORE-us), meaning "thickheaded lizard," named for the extremely thick bone between the brain and outer surface on the top of its head. It was believed to walk upright with long hind legs and shorter front legs. No complete skeletons have been discovered yet, but it is estimated at 15 feet long and larger. Its snout was decorated with a variety of bony spikes, and the back of the head with pointed nodules. Its brain was smaller than that of a sheep and was encased in a skull of solid bone. The male had a head bone up to 10 inches thick, while the female's head bone was believed to be slightly thinner.

The 26-inch-long skulls were designed to transfer impact through the dome around the sides of the head and backbone. Its backbone could be held in a horizontal position. Its short neck apparently could be moved up or down and be held in a battering position as shown by how the backbones fit together in a stiff fortifying manner. Its joints between the backbone and skull had special grooves which prevented twisting. Some believe it butted other *Pachycephalosaurs*, as do big horn sheep to compete for mates and territories. Another possibility is that it butted trees down to eat the leaves, as do rhinoceros today.

Assorted *Hadrosaurs*

Hadrosaurs (HAD-roh-sores)

The *Hadrosaurs* were duck-billed dinosaurs, huge herbivores with toothless bills followed by what seemed like endless rows of teeth, sometimes up to 2000 of them! It had more teeth than any other dinosaur. These diamond-shaped teeth were unevenly distributed in the jaw, with some higher than others. The jaws were designed for grinding, and when they were brought together, they had a mill-like effect. New teeth replaced the old worn-out ones in this very complicated dental arrangement. Some believe these bills were used to probe water plants, as ducks use their similarly-shaped bills today.

There were three basic groups of *Hadrosaurs*: flat-headed, solid-crested, and hollow-crested. They were bird-hipped and bird-footed, with three toes forward and one toe back. They were believed to stand upright on their longer hind legs and stood on all fours using their shorter forelimbs when foraging or browsing low to the ground. Their long tails helped them keep their 26 to 33-foot-long bodies in balance. It is believed they spent much of their time in the water and could have had webbed feet, but this is speculation.

Flat-Headed Hadrosaurs

Edmontosaurs (ed-mont-oh-SORE-us) were flat-headed *Hadrosaurs*, named for Edmonton, the area in Canada where they were first found. They were the largest *Hadrosaurs*, growing up to 43 feet long and weighing an estimated 3-3½ tons. They are one of the best-understood dinosaurs because so many well-preserved fossils have been found. Fossils found in Wyoming, USA actually showed the impression of leathery skin with a round or oval bumpy design similar to the Gila monster or the surface of a basketball. Apparently it did not have any armor or hard scales. The mud evidently formed a mold around the dinosaur's head, shoulders, forelimbs, legs, and tail so quickly that the dinosaur didn't have time to decay.

Edmontosaurus was similar to *Iguanodon* in shape, but it had a duck-bill and did not have spiked thumbs. It had short thick legs with 3 widely separated toes. It had a broad snout and large eyes and was believed to have nostrils on the top of its rather flat head, but this is speculation. Many believe it had loose, inflatable skin surrounding its nostrils and down the front of its face. It had 1000 teeth!

Saurolophus

Solid-Crested Hadrosaurs

Saurolophus (sore-roh-LOAF-us) and *Maiasaurus* (my-ah-SORE-us) were solid-crested *Hadrosaurs*. The *Saurolophus* was 30-35 feet long and similar to an *Edmontosaurus*, except it had a shorter, narrower bill and a solid low flat crest, making it the least conspicuous of the crested *Hadrosaurs*. The discovery of the sclerotic rings (a type of connective tissue around the eyes) near fossil bones indicate to paleontologists that *Saurolophus'* eyes were much smaller than the eye sockets they filled.

Maiasaurus, meaning "good mother lizard," had a small solid crest in the form of a short spike protruding forward from above the eyes and a toothless beak followed by hundreds of cheek teeth. Its body was shaped like *Edmontosaurus* but smaller at 25-30 feet long. It is currently one of the most popular dinosaurs due to the traveling exhibit of Dr. Jack Horner and associates and the children's books written about their extensive findings.

Jack Horner's enlightening discovery included eggs, juveniles, and adults. For the first time, something of the physical development and family life of dinosaurs could be interpreted from the fossils. Since 1978, Dr. Horner has found more than 500 whole and partial eggs still in the nests. For the first time, eggs containing embryos were found. *Maiasaurs* laid their eggs in a circular pattern like the spokes on a wheel. The nests were spaced one adult body length apart. The adults evidently provided all the needs of the hatchlings and continued to care for the juveniles, which is seen by the crushed eggshells and fossil hatchlings up to 20 inches long still in the nests.

In other types of fossil dinosaur nests, eggs were slightly broken on one end where hatchlings exited the egg. In cases where the young inhabited the nest for extended periods, such as the *Maiasaurs*, the eggs were found

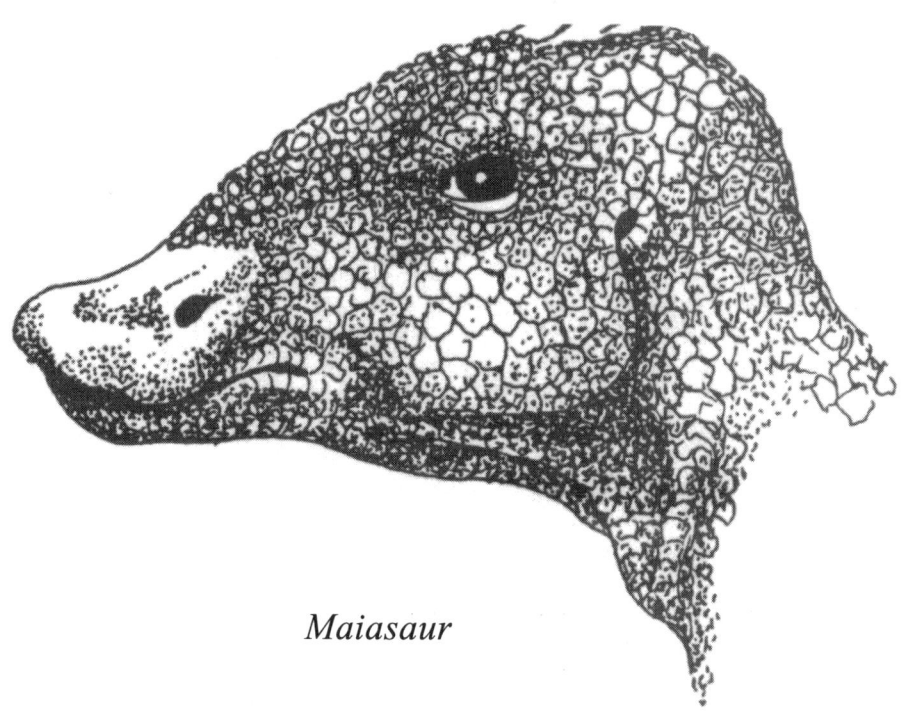

Maiasaur

crushed, stomped underfoot. It is believed that *Maiasaurs* took care of their young for the first year, and that they doubled their body weight each year for the first four years. Apparently juveniles longer than 3 feet long were still cared for by the parents and thus the name "good mother lizards."

Jack Horner's *Maiasaur* exhibit was particularly good for several reasons. The parts of the fossils which had actually been found were displayed in one color, and the parts which were added or speculated were displayed in another color. Given along with the paleontologist's interpretations was the fossil evidence from which the interpretations were made. This allowed individuals to decide for themselves how the evidence might be explained, which for a creationist is a welcome change.

An estimated 10,000 *Maiasaurs* were discovered in the deepest layer of sediments. Jack Horner says, "We had one huge bed of *Maiasaur* bones — and nothing but *Maiasaur* bones — stretching a mile and a quarter east to west and a quarter-mile north to south." From the evidence, Jack Horner and his group believe they were killed by a volcanic eruption and then buried by a "catastrophic inundation." This huge herd of *Maiasaurs* was probably killed by the opening of the fountains of the deep, which involved worldwide volcanic activity, and then buried under the sediments carried by the incoming Floodwaters. (For more information on this, refer to Appendix B Parts 3-5.) Jack Horner does not believe in the Bible or the world-covering Genesis Flood.

Fossil dinosaurs, nests, and eggs were found on three separate horizons, or layers of rock, above the huge Flood-deposited herd. Local flooding during the post-Flood Ice Age, along with radically changing sea levels, would easily explain these deposits. (Refer to Appendix B Parts 6-7 for further information.)

Hollow-Crested Hadrosaurs

Hollow-crested *Hadrosaurs* are the *Lambeosaurs* (LAM-bee-oh-sores), meaning "Lambe's lizard." *Corythosaurus* (coh-rith-oh-SORE-us), meaning "helmet lizard," had a hollow half-disk-shaped bony crest that started just above the beak and extended to the back of its head. The complex system of tubes in the crest is believed to have been air passages that extended from the nostrils on the bill through the crest and exited into the back of the throat. The crest of the male is believed to have been more prominent than that of the female. It was 18-33 feet long, is estimated at 2-4 tons, had pebble or basketball-like skin, and was decorated with three rows of nodules around its belly.

The particular *Hadrosaur*, *Lambeosaurus*, was named in honor of Canadian paleontologist Lawrence Lambe. This was the largest *Ornithischian* or bird-hipped dinosaur at 30-49 feet long and 8 feet high at the hip. Its narrow nose ended in a broad blunt beak. Its hollow hatchet-shaped crest started at its nose and rose high above its eyes, with a pointed handle extending backwards from its skull, which appears to be a combination of crests of the *Corythosaurus* and the *Saurolophus*. Its body shape was like the *Saurolophus*, but its legs were shorter and more powerful, so they are believed to have been faster runners than the other *Hadrosaurs*. Its skin lacked little bumps and nodules like the *Corythosaurus* had. Could it have been a cross of these two variations within kind?

The large cavity in its hatchet-like crest was connected to the nasal passage, leading scientists to believe the hollow crests were used to amplify sounds; they also believe the males had the larger crests. *Lambeosaurs* apparently populated North America in abundance.

Tsintaosaurus (sin-taow-SORE-us), considered the unicorn of dinosaurs, was a hollow-crested *Hadrosaur* named for the location where it was found in China in 1958. Its crest was believed to be skin covered and shaped like a spike or a blade-like horn pointing forward from between its eyes. Being hollow, it is believed to have had tubes running through it.

Parasaurolophus (par-ah-sore-oh-LOAF-us), meaning "like crested lizard," was probably the most conspicuous *Hadrosaur* because it had the largest crest. Its hollow crest was a long curved bony tube which extended well behind its head and was 3-6 feet long on a 5 ton, 30 to 33-foot-long dinosaur. Some believe this crest was used like a snorkel, but others disagree because there doesn't appear to be an opening to the lungs. Some fossil evidence shows a sphincter muscle may have existed in the *Hadrosaur's* crest to close the air passage when the creature submerged, similar to those in crocodiles, otters, and hippopotami.

The crest could have been for vocalization. Paleontologist Dr. Weishampel theorizes that vocalization through its huge crest was so annoying to those listening, that it might have been a means of defense. *Parasaurolophus* had an unusually large optic lobe, optic nerve, and eyeballs, indicating that it might have had very good vision. It also had a rather unique tail, broad and flattened on two sides. It too was abundant in North America.

Parasaurolophus

Part Three

Pterosaur (TAIR-oh-sores)

Flying reptiles are *Pterosaurs*, meaning "winged lizards." Its wings, covered in skin rather than feathers, extended from its body to the end of its extremely long fourth finger, its 'wing-finger.' Its bones were delicate and full of air spaces, designed to be light, yet strong. It is believed to be carnivorous. Whether *Pterosaurs* were warm- or cold-blooded is an ongoing debate. Birds are warm-blooded and have very high metabolisms to supply the energy required to fly. Scientists don't believe cold-blooded animals could have produced enough energy for flight. *Pterosaurs* came in two basic kinds: the shorter-necked **Rhamphorhynchus** (ram-foh-RINK-us) and the longer-necked, long-headed **Pterodactyl** (tair-oh-DAK-tul), meaning "winged fingers."

Short-necked *Rhamphorhynchus* had a beak full of sharp teeth, which pointed forward and stuck out, even when its beak was closed. Its tail, possibly used as a rudder, ended in a kite shape called a tail vane. Its 2-foot-long body was carried on 6-foot-long wings giving it a 12-foot wingspan.

Among the *Pterodactyls*, most had teeth, but not **Pteranodons** (tair-AN-oh-don). Their name means "winged and toothless." Scientists believe this flying lizard, having ranged from a 23 to 30 foot wingspan, was designed to glide more than fly, similar to an albatross. A bony crest extended back, crowning its elongated toothless skull attached to its 3-foot, 45-pound body by a snake-like neck. One specimen measured 5 feet 9 inches from the end of its beak to the tip of its crest! Scientists thought the crest was used somehow in the aerodynamics of flight. Now it is believed to have been a counterbalance for the weight of its long beak.

The largest known animal to ever fly was the *Pterodactyl* **Quetzalcoatlus** (ket-sol-koh-AT-lus), named for the Aztec god Quetzalcoatl. In 1972, its fossil was discovered in Big Bend National Park, Texas. It had a 39-foot wingspan, wider than the wingspan of many jets. The creature is believed to have weighed only 190 pounds.

In 1970, a Russian paleontologist, Professor Sharov, reported finding a very well preserved slab, including delicate leaves, insects, and a small, extremely well-preserved *Pterosaur* complete with impressions of wing membranes and a furry covering! Sharov says the creature was covered in long, thick fur all over its body and even had tufts of longer hair in places that curved and bent in the fossil. He named the creature *Sordes pilosus*, which can be translated as "filthy fur" or "hairy devil." Today's reptiles do not have hair. If some *Pterosaurs* did have hair, it could open up some interesting questions, such as these. Did other reptiles in the past have hair? Were they warm-blooded like living creatures with hair? Were all *Pterosaurs* flying mammals, similar to bats, or was *Sordes pilosus* actually the fossil of some extinct flying mammal and not a *Pterosaur* at all?

69

Part Four

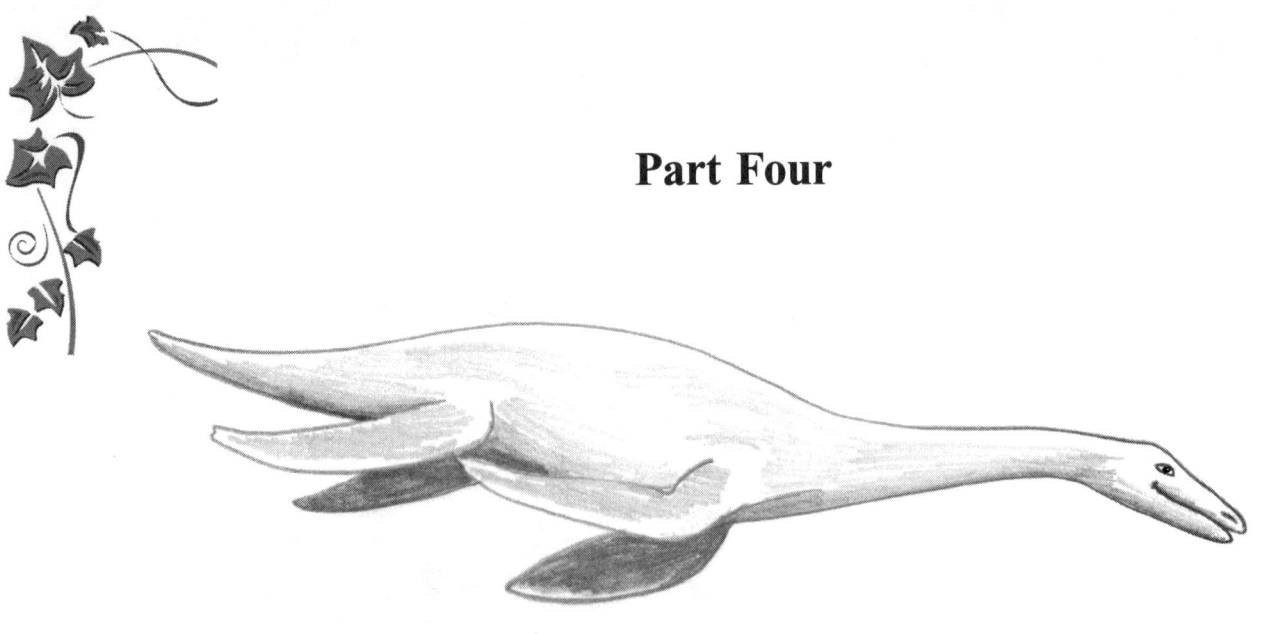

Sea Dragons

Though **Archelon** (AR-kee-lon), the gigantic 14-foot-long sea turtle, was a huge marine reptile, it will not be included here because sea turtles are still fairly common today and don't fit our dragon designation.

Plesiosaurs (PLEE-see-oh-sores) had long necks and small heads full of sharp teeth. Four large flippers powered its oblong body, which ranged from 7 to 46 feet in length. One type of *Plesiosaur,* the **Elasmosaur** (ee-LAS-moh-sore), had a neck that accounted for more than half of its length, which could be up to 43 feet long. Paleontologists suggest that they may have waddled on their flippers to come out of the water at times. This is supported by some eyewitness sightings of lake dragons on land. (See Chapter 9.)

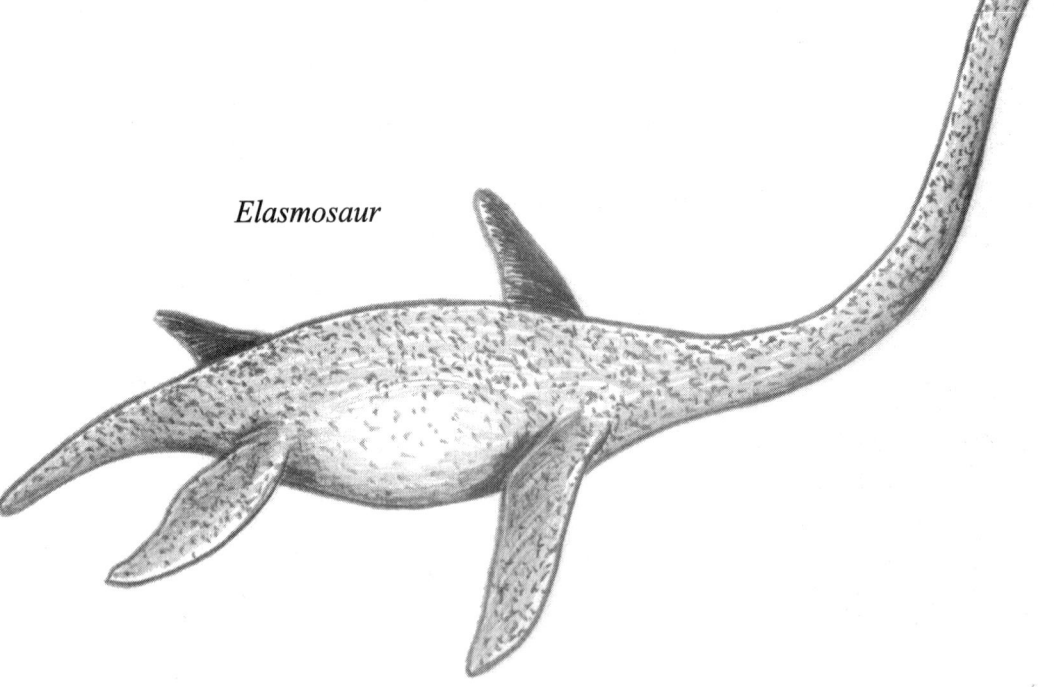

Elasmosaur

Pliosaurs (ply-oh-SORES) had shorter, thicker necks and longer, larger heads than *Plesiosaurs*. The *Pliosaur* **Peloneustes** (pel-o-NEWS-tees), found in Western Europe, was relatively small at 10 feet long with four flippers, a short neck, and a long skull about 1/4 the length of its body. It apparently ate, or at least bit, ammonites (coiled marine mollusks) because fossil ammonite shells pierced with *Peloneustes* teeth have been found. Another *Pliosaur* was **Kronosaurus** (kroh-noh-SORE-us), a 56-foot-long terror of the ocean. Its 10-foot-wide mouth was filled with massive, sharp front teeth and 10-inch-long bullet-shaped rear teeth, possibly used for crushing mollusks.

Ichthyosaurs (ICK-thee-oh-sores) were the dolphins of the reptile world. They were believed to be acrobatic, like dolphins, with their fins, flippers, and streamlined 10-foot-long bodies. From the fossil record, we know they gave birth to live young. One *Ichthyosaur* was buried so rapidly that her fossil reveals that half of her baby was still in the birth canal and half was out of her body. This is good evidence of rapid burial.

Opthalmosaurus (op-thal-moh-SORE-us) was a 12-foot-long *Ichthyosaur* with saucer-sized eyes in its 3½-foot-long head. **Shonisaurus** (show-nih-SORE-us) was the largest known *Ichthyosaur* at 50 feet long. It had teeth only in the front of its long narrow mouth.

Ammonite

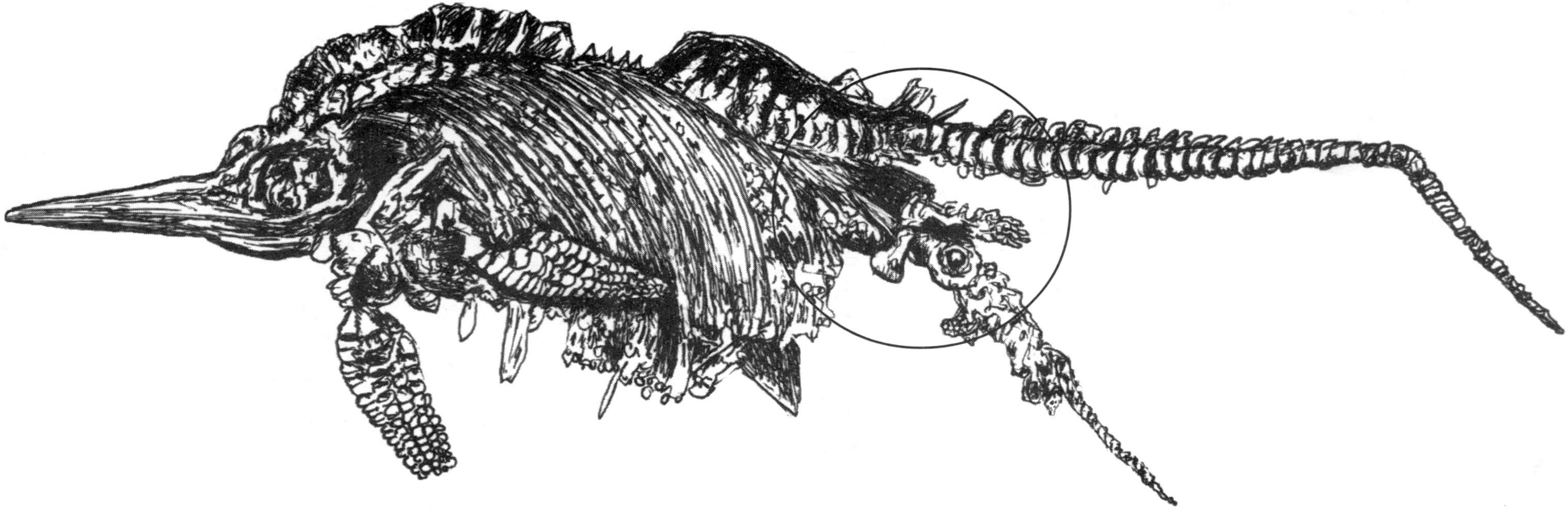

Ichthyosaur fossilized while giving birth

Chapter Five

Enter Jehovah's Park

Enter Jehovah's Park

Requirements to Enter Jehovah's Park

To enter **Jehovah's Park**, you need more than a helicopter ride to an island off the coast of Costa Rica (which was the location of *Jurassic Park* in the movie). You need a Bible and a basic knowledge of the creation interpretation of natural history, so . . . Grab your Bible and keep reading! I'll help you put on those Biblical Spectacles so you can finally pull back the curtain veiling the secrets of Jehovah's Park.

When natural history is viewed through our Biblical Spectacles, all life on earth started around 6000 years ago. On the fifth day of the Creation Week, all the winged and sea creatures were created, including *Pterosaurs, Plesiosaurs*, and *Pliosaurs*. On the sixth day, all the land creatures were created, including the *Carnosaurs, Ceratopsids,* and *Sauropods*. They were all created to be vegetarians, because originally, God's world was perfect. Death did not exist for anything with the breath of life in it (Hebrew *nephesh*) until after man sinned, and all creation went under the curse of death.

The world became so violent that God sent the first judgment, the Genesis Flood, which covered all dry land and erased the pre-Flood world by erosion. The Flood, which occurred around 2350 B.C., and its aftereffects deposited the vast majority of sedimentary rocks and fossils worldwide. The one Ice Age that the world experienced was an aftereffect of the Flood. It caused radically different global sea levels and rapid climate changes to occur. Habitats changed from mild to harsh causing many larger creatures, including dinosaurs and their enemies, the mammoths and elephants, to become extinct in certain areas. Appendix B contains a more thorough presentation of the creation interpretation of natural history for those who desire more information.

Dinosaurs and Dragons in the Bible

As we re-enter our adventure after the Flood, the past 4,350 years, it is important to remember that before the 1840's, these ravenous reptiles went by many different names. We finally get to explore some of these aliases. Some of the more common dinosaur aliases before the 1840's were the names serpent, monster, and dragon.

I believe that dinosaurs lived before and after the Flood and were aboard Noah's Ark because of various Biblical references to strange creatures fitting the dinosaurs' descriptions. For example, **Behemoth** is found in Job 40:15-24 and is described as "*chief in the ways of God.*" (Refer to Appendix B Part 3 for information on how dinosaurs and all the other land animals could have fit on the Ark.) Some would like us to believe that **Behemoth** was an elephant or a hippopotamus. In Job 40:17, the movement of **Behemoth**'s tail is compared to a cedar. Cedar trees were coveted in the ancient world and were known to be huge. If you look at the tail of the elephant or hippo, you'll see that they have wimpy little stick-sized tails, not like cedar trees! Some study Bibles want us to believe that the cedar-tree description is of the elephant's trunk. I think God knows the difference between a nose and a tail, don't you?!

We learn from Biblical eyewitness observation that **Behemoth** ate grass like an ox, had bones like strong pieces of brass, and limbs like bars of iron. He rested under the willows, and in the reeds and marshes. Raging river waters weren't a problem for him, so he must have been right at home in the water. I believe these verses are a great description of a *Sauropod* very shortly after the Flood.

While you're in Job, have some real fun; read the 41st chapter and learn about the fire-breathing, possibly amphibious dragon, **Leviathan**. He was very strong, and "*around his teeth there [was] terror.*" His scales were as strong as armor fitted so tightly together that air didn't get through. Even swords, spears, darts, and a coat of armor were worthless against him; his hide was so strong that iron was as straw and bronze as rotten wood. Job 41:18-21 says,

> *His sneezes flash forth light,*
> *And his eyes are like the eyelids of the morning.*
> *Out of his mouth go burning torches;*
> *Sparks of fire leap forth.*
> *Out of his nostrils smoke goes forth,*
> *As from a boiling pot and burning rushes.*
> *His breath kindles coals, And a flame goes forth from his mouth.*

There really were fire-breathing dragons. It's not just mythology or people's overactive imaginations!

Behemoth

Leviathan

Leviathan is not the only fire-breathing reptile mentioned in the Bible. Isaiah 14:29 and 30:6 make reference to a "***fiery-flying serpent.***" In the Middle Ages serpents referred to reptiles and included those with legs. The *fiery flying serpent* must have been a reptile, now extinct, possibly a *Pterosaur* of some sort, and thank God they're extinct! Descriptions of fire-breathing flying serpents are found in various ancient writings and some in fairly recent accounts. These are discussed further in Chapter 7.

Are you aware that there are still fire-blowing bugs living today? They're called bombardier beetles, or among horse people and in some southern states in the USA, they're referred to as "blister beetles." Their defense mechanism is to shoot hot chemicals out of two little exhaust pipes on their back-end. If the beetle is on you when it shoots its chemical, you are left with a mean blister from the burn, thus the name. There are still fire-blowing bugs, so the idea of fire-breathing dragons shouldn't be so incredible.

In the Old Testament, the Hebrew word *tanniyn* (or *tanniym*) is found at least 27 times. It was translated monster, whale or sea-serpent, jackal or other hideous land animal, serpent or dragon. In the KJV, it was frequently translated serpent or dragon.

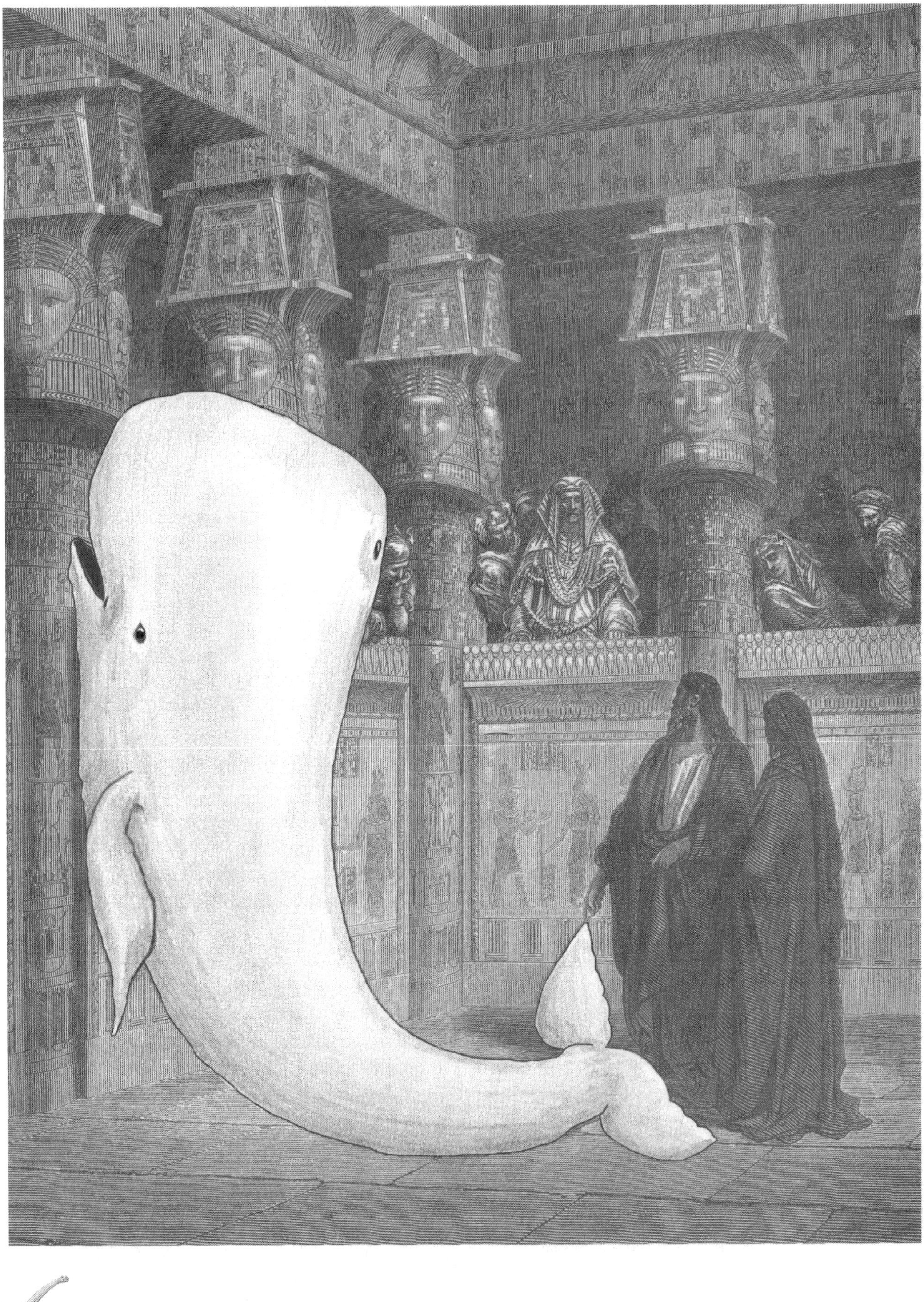

A well-known story from Exodus, thanks to Hollywood's *The Ten Commandments* and *Prince of Egypt*, is Moses going before Pharaoh to demand that he "let the children of Israel go" (KJV). In this account, Aaron, Moses' older brother and spokesman, did as the Lord commanded and cast down his rod before Pharaoh and his court. It turned into a serpent. Pharaoh responded by having his magicians do the same. Then God's serpent swallowed Pharaoh's serpents. In the Hebrew, the rods turned into *tanniyn*, so the rods probably turned into dragons.

In Genesis 1:21, God created the great sea *tanniym* or sea monsters. The KJV translated this passage as God created the great whales. (In the 1600's English the word "whale" apparently included many large non-mammalian marine creatures or sea monsters. Today, the word whale specifically refers to large marine mammals.) If the Hebrew word *tanniym* actually was referring to a large marine mammal, then Pharaoh and his court really got a surprise! Can you just picture a whale waddling over Pharaoh's highly polished floor to swallow his magician's whales? Monster or dragon definitely seems to be the better current interpretation for *tanniyn* in Exodus 7.

In the NIV, *tanniym* was translated to "jackal." Dr. Charles V. Taylor, a professional linguist, explains, "it seems the NIV went to the supposed root *tannah*, 'howl' for its interpretation. Noting the context of dry or derelict places . . . , they regarded the jackal as a more likely 'howler' than any dinosaur, if only because they did not believe such creatures would be alive then."[7a]

Many believe dinosaurs made howling noises after studying how the bones in their skulls were formed as previously discussed in the *Hadrosaur* section. **Grendel** (GRRRAIN-dall with a rolled "r"), an Old English name for a particular bipedal (upright walking) dragon, comes from the Old Norse word *grenja* (GRRRAIN-hah) which meant bellow, growl, or howl.[7b]

In the Septuagint, the Greek word from which the English word "siren" is derived is translated twice into the English as "dragon." The Oxford English Dictionary relates that the original meaning of "siren" from Homer's Odyssey was:

> An imaginary species of serpent; one of several fabulous monsters, part woman, part bird, who were supposed to lure sailors to their destruction by their enchanting singing; the mud-iguana . . . Native to North America.

Linnaeus, the father of modern taxonomy or biological classification systems, was told the mud iguana, mentioned above, "had a sort of singing voice." From the historical evidence, it appears reptiles were capable of howling.[8]

The Bible reveals that some dragons were venomous as in Deuteronomy 32:33 "the poison of dragons." Psalms 140:3 says adders were also venomous. Adders are usually portrayed to us today as venomous snakes. The 1828 Webster's Dictionary defines an adder as "a venomous serpent or viper, of several species." Interestingly, the next word in this dictionary is ***adder***fly, which is another name for the ***dragon***fly. Considering dragons were frequently called serpents in the early times, could adders have originally referred to venomous dragons?

The most mysterious serpent in the KJV Bible is the **Cockatrice** found in Isaiah 11:8, 14:29, 59:5, and Jeremiah 8:17. We know they existed because of their description in the Bible, but their attributes have been greatly embellished through time, so it is difficult to know what the real creature was like. The 1828 Webster's Dictionary defines the **Cockatrice** as "A serpent imagined to proceed from a cock's egg." This 1828 dictionary relates that the cockatrice was also known as a **Basilisk** or "king-serpent." In the original Greek it meant "little king" due to their head structure and ability to kill other serpents. The 1828 dictionary specifically defines the **Basilisk** as:

> A fabulous serpent, called a cockatrice, and said to be produced from a cock's egg brooded by a serpent. The ancients alledged that its hissing would drive away all other serpents, and that its breath and even its look was fatal. Some writers suppose that a real serpent exists under this name.

Notice that some suppose a real serpent "exists," present tense in this definition, as late as 1828.

Basilisks (**Cockatrices**) are found in histories from ancient times until fairly recent accounts, as are other dragons. In the historical account, they are described as the most deadly of serpents, which also contributes to the king-serpent designation. It supposedly came from the egg laid by a seven-year-old rooster during the time of the star Sirius being high in the heavens. Its egg was described as spherical and covered by a thick membrane. It was said to be incubated for a longer than normal time, sometimes by a serpent, and at other times by a toad.

The adult **Basilisk** was described as cat-size with the body and legs of a rooster, the tail and head of a snake, and the eyes of a toad. It was said to be so venomous that even its breath was absolutely lethal and would bring pestilence to the area in which it lived. The danger of this creature was exaggerated until its very look was said to be fatal, even to itself; therefore, carrying a mirror to shine its reflection back on it was believed the only safe way to kill one. The weasel was its only known natural enemy.

This mythical view cannot possibly be an accurate portrayal of the actual animal, but from these accounts we can hypothesize what the real **Cockatrice** might have been like, and because it's mentioned in the Bible as a real animal, it's a worthy endeavor.

The myth said the **Cockatrice** egg was laid during the time of Sirius. This might have been a reference to the season in which the animal laid its eggs. It was said to be the egg of a rooster, and we all know that roosters don't lay eggs! The **Cockatrice** egg was probably similar in size to a chicken egg, but it was circular instead of ovoid, and it had a tough membrane instead of a hard shell. Not surprisingly, this is a good scientific description of a reptile egg. The creature that hatched out of this strange egg had some rooster-like characteristics: the rooster's body, legs, and feet. Between the egg looking like a malformed chicken egg and the offspring resembling a rooster, it's not hard to see why some might have thought it was a rooster's egg.

The **Cockatrice** egg was said to be brooded (incubated) by a snake or toad. This is probably because the creature which hatched out was described as having the head and tail of a snake and the eyes of a toad.

The **Cockatrice**'s fatally-venomous breath could be explained by the creature being able to spit its venom, like a cobra can. The weasel was said to be its natural enemy and the mongoose is still known to be the natural enemy of many venomous reptiles.

Using our Biblical Spectacles and knowing that dinosaurs and man lived at the same time allows us to look for a dragon or dinosaur that fits the historical description. One candidate is the *Podokesaurus*. From the fossils, it appears to have been the height of a large housecat with the body and legs of a rooster and the tail and head of a serpent.

  If the **Cockatrice** was winged, then it was some kind of *Pterosaur*. Prosper Alpin, an outstanding naturalist of the 16th century, explicitly described the **Basilisk** as being a flying serpent with a head crest and tail vane that still lived in Ethiopia.[9] We can determine something of the way the **Cockatrice** may have looked from its fossils, but through the historical description of the **Basilisk**, we can also surmise that it might have been highly venomous and even able to spit its venom. (This was an ability given to one of the small bipedal dinosaurs in the first *Jurassic Park* movie.) It could have been a venomous *Pterosaur* with toad-like eyes. We can't know for sure, but the mystery is worth exploring. There is still a species of crested lizard today that is called a *Basilisk* in remembrance of this creature.

Actual engravings and woodcuts of Basilisks from books of the 1300 to 1600's

Isaiah 11:8 shares a glimpse of God's peace, which will be restored to the earth someday when the wolf shall dwell with the lamb. We get a new appreciation for the level of danger that will be removed from the earth when the weaned child puts his hand on the den of the **Cockatrice** (KJV), a much more dangerous animal than the viper found in the NASV and NIV. The Amplified Bible translates this as an adder. If adder meant venomous dragon, then it would sound more like the dangerous dragon description given historically to this beast.

A knight attempting to kill a Basilisk with its own reflection

Chapter Six

Land Dragons and Man

Land Dragons and Man

Secular History

Many people find historical accounts of dragons and monsters to be unbelievable at best. They want the scientific facts, not hearsay reports and exaggerated legends; but even some legends are based in fact. If land dragons were dinosaurs and these historical accounts are true, they support the Jehovah's Park idea that man lived alongside dinosaurs. Eyewitness observations of living dinosaurs could also give us insight into the details about these mysterious creatures, which are the subject of debates, such as whether *Tyrannosaurs* were predators or not.

General curiosities could be answered, such as what color they were, who or what they ate, and whether they had webbed feet? Those of us who are not convinced that dinosaurs died off millions of years ago can have great fun exploring these accounts, gleaning otherwise unknowable details about these creatures. Those who are skeptical might be surprised at the amount of historical evidence that exists and is regularly ignored. Secular history is full of dragons, sea serpents, flying serpents, and fire-breathing dragons. The following chapter represents only a sampling of these accounts.

Historically, people gave specific names to particular types of dragons to more easily identify them; thus, dinosaurs had many aliases. Most secular books that contain collections of historical dragon sightings admit that dinosaur fossils with flesh and skin added would definitely produce reptiles fitting the dragon descriptions. They usually go on to say that modern science (science through Naturalistic Spectacles) has shown that man and dinosaurs were separated by millions of years, so dragons could not be dinosaurs. Due to the Naturalistic perspective, the dinosaurs' demise continues to be one of the greatest unsolved mysteries of our time.

If you'll put on your Biblical Spectacles as you read the following historical accounts and quotes, you might find the solution to this great mystery as well as another: *what were the dinosaurs really like*? From these accounts we can surmise many things about their dispositions, habits, and even colors, which could be learned only through eyewitness observations.

Chinese Dragons

Chinese history, the longest continuous secular history of any nation, tells of a world-covering Flood and is full of dragons. Shortly after the division of nations at the Tower of Babel (described in Genesis 11 and discussed in light of the Ice Age in Appendix B, Part 7), one family bred dragons to sell to the Chinese Emperor, who used them to pull his chariots in parades. In 1611 B.C., the Emperor of China appointed the first Royal Dragon Feeder, which remained an honored post for many years afterward. According to Buddhist records, the practice of feeding dragons was common throughout the Orient. There was one dragon chapel on the Indus River where a copper vessel was kept filled with cream to feed the dragons.[10]

Unlike the description of western dragons, eastern dragons rarely had wings and are described as breathing clouds, not fire. Their voices were reported to sound like jingling coins, ringing bells, and clanging gongs.[11] Though they were known to be hot-tempered and killed people at times, they are never said to have eaten anyone.[12] Dragon skin was said to glow in the dark, not unlike fireflies, and when dragon fat was burned, the flames were visible for hundreds of miles. Their spittle (saliva) was used to make the rarest perfumes and the most permanent dyes.[13]

Dragon meat was reserved for royal kitchens. During a storm, a dragon was reportedly killed on palace grounds, which Emperor Hwo ordered to be made into soup. He and his ministers enjoyed the royal broth. Emperor Chao (1085-1135 A.D.) caught a tusked dragon while fishing in the Wei River and delivered it to his chefs to be prepared.[14]

As late as the Sung Dynasty (960-1279 A.D.), the saliva of the purple dragon was said to be used to inscribe the names of the most honored ministers and their stories on tablets of jade, gold, and crystal. Marco Polo was in China at this time and reported seeing them. To have a ready supply, the purple dragons were raised in the palace compound. It is recorded that the dragon's favorite food was roasted sparrows. When its saliva was needed, roasted sparrows were waved under its nose, and the dragon would drool.[15]

The royal dragon always had five toes, while the people's dragons had four. Fossils have shown that some *Sauropods* had five toes, and some had four. Most are described as walking down on all fours and being reasonably friendly. From these descriptions, possibly the herbivorous *Sauropods* or *Stegasaurs* made their home rather successfully in the Orient.

The Chinese used dragons for medicinal purposes from ancient times until as late as the 16th century A.D. as seen in a prescription narrative **Pan Ts'ai Kang Mu**. Many of the medical treatments used bone remains and soft tissue, which required freshly killed dragon parts, not fossils.[16] Ground spine was used to cure gallstones, infantile fever, paralysis of the legs, and ailments of pregnant women. Teeth were used in the treatment of headaches and madness. Brain and liver were used against dysentery.

Whole villages supported themselves by digging up and selling dragon bones, until 1927, when visiting scientists from the American Museum of Natural History claimed dragon bones were the fossil remains of prehistoric animals. They purchased many of these bones and shipped them to museums back in the USA. Afterwards, it became illegal for the Chinese people to dig and sell dragon bones.[17]

A Chinese teacher saw a cow-headed dragon on the shore of the Yellow River in the 1920's. He described the dragon as being bright blue and as big as five cows. The dragon crawled into the water when it started to rain.[18]

These are just a small sample of the many Chinese dragon sightings and reports. The next time you go into a Chinese restaurant, notice the dragons.

If you were to look up the word dragon in the *Chinese-English Dictionary* (published in 1979), you would read:

1. dragon,
2. imperial (as in imperial robe),
3. huge extinct reptile: dinosaur,
4. a surname.

This dictionary acknowledges clearly that dragons were dinosaurs. The Chinese character (written symbol) for "dinosaur" is pronounced "konglong," which translates literally to "fearsome dragon." Many traditional Chinese sayings connect dragons with real animals, especially the tiger: "a coiling dragon and crouching tiger" means a forbidding strategic point, "dragon's pool and tiger's den" means a dangerous place, and "dragons rising and tigers leaping" means a scene of bustling activity. These sayings give a rather formidable feeling about dragons. Animal symbols are used to represent the twelve lunar cycles in the Chinese calendar. Eleven of them are animals familiar to us today. The twelfth is the dragon, which evidently was also a real animal familiar to those individuals who originally assigned the symbols.[19] Evidently, at least some Chinese acknowledged that dragons were dinosaurs, not just mythical creatures!

Other Eastern Dragons

Historical dragon reports show up in many other cultures also. They have long been ignored or assumed to be fictitious, because evolution teaches that man never saw living dinosaurs; thus, dragons are usually treated as mythology. When viewed as historical accounts, interesting observations can be gleaned about these mysterious monsters.

In the 300's B.C., Alexander the Great advanced into India. It is recorded that many animals, including monstrous serpents, were found. The Indian people still worshiped these huge hissing reptiles that lived in caves.[20]

The flightless **Lindworm** was reported to have a snake-like body with only one pair of large hind legs that were easily seen. It may have been a bipedal (upright-walking) dinosaur with short forelimbs, which might not have been seen by people who were, understandably, keeping their distance. The Italian explorer Marco Polo reported seeing **Lindworms** while crossing the Steppes (great plains) of Central Asia.[21]

The city of Cracow was named after Cracus (c. 700 A.D.), who reportedly slew an immense dragon that had made its lair in a crag.[22]

Draco bipes apteros captus in Agro Bononiensi.

Actual engraving of a Lindworm

Dragons in the Epic Poem "Beowulf"

The Anglo-Saxon poem about Beowulf is full of reptilian monsters. Beowulf was born in 495 A.D., and was a king of the tribe Geatingas, which inhabited what is now southern Sweden. Many modern translators attempt to call these reptilian monsters trolls. Bill Cooper is an expert on the Old English (Anglo-Saxon Celtic) language, history, and translation of genealogies and documents. In his book *After the Flood*, Cooper states that neither trolls, nor fairies, nor giants, nor dwarfs of any kind are mentioned anywhere in the Beowulf epic.[23] Instead, this poem references a variety of animals whose descriptions fit *Theropods* (bipedal carnivorous dinosaurs), *Pterosaurs* (flying reptiles), sea dragons, lake dragons, and a stag (a large male deer).[24]

Beowulf battling Grendel

The word **Grendel** was used in the Beowulf epic as the common name for a *Theropod* that sounds suspiciously like a *Tyrannosaur*. It was bipedal with small and comparatively weak forelimbs, also referred to as claws. The name given this creature is very reminiscent of the deep-throated growl that a very large animal would make. It came into Middle English usage meaning "angry." Danish nicknames given to this **Grendel** were ominous, such as "God's adversary," "evil-doer," "damned," "devil in hell," and "hellish monster descended from Cain himself."[25] These names give us some idea of the disposition of this beast.

It reportedly hunted alone and would approach villages at night to look for prey, often devouring the unfortunate Danish guard who was employed to warn the villagers of the monster's approach. One particular long-remembered night, **Grendel** killed 30 Danish warriors.

Beowulf was able to kill the juvenile male **Grendel** that had been terrorizing the Danish people for 12 years. He avoided its deadly jaws by coming in close to the animal's torso and wrenching off its tiny forelimb, causing it to retreat and die from its wounds.[26]

The name **Grendel** is not unique to the Beowulf epic but is found as a generic term for dragons in Old English as late as the 10th century. King Athelstan of Wessex in 931 A.D. referred to a certain lake in Wiltshire as **Grendles mere** (a mere being a small pond or lake). Old English charters refer to other places as **Grindles bec** and **Grendeles pyt**. In Switzerland there is **Grindelwald** meaning literally **Grendelwood**.[27]

Other creatures described in the epic include sea dragons (called **Saedracan**) and monsters of the lakes. They were responsible for many deaths and could be regularly seen sunning themselves, but would quickly slither back into the water when they heard danger approaching. In one instance, Beowulf and his men reportedly killed one, harpooned it, and pulled it out to examine its body. Beowulf was known to have cleared the sea routes between Denmark and Sweden of these monsters. On one particularly successful expedition, Beowulf and his men displayed 9 carcasses on the beach to entertain and impress the local people[28].

Several flying reptiles were described in literature from this period, including **Lyftfloga** meaning "air-flier," and **Widfloga**, meaning "far-ranging flier," whose description fits that of a giant *Pteranodon*. **Ligdraca**, meaning "fire-dragon," is described as being about 300 years old (great age is common today in reptiles) and having a length of 50 feet (possibly describing its wingspan). The last monster Beowulf killed was a flying reptile, which lived on a high-ridge overlooking the sea on what is now the southern coast of Sweden. This last battle took place in 583 A.D. when the old dragon fighter was 88 years old! He later died from wounds received in this battle.[29]

European and Western Dragons

Pliny the Elder, a first century Roman naturalist and author of the 37-volume *Natural History*, tells of a dragon killed on Vatican Hill during the reign of Emperor Claudius who died in 54 A.D. The body of a child was found in the beast. Pliny the Elder also recorded uses for dragon's teeth and the fat of dragon's heart. He describes ointments made from dried dragon's eyes and honey, and other such remedies.[30]

The **Heraldic Dragon** was reportedly very formidable: a dragon with massive fangs, four clawed feet, and a ridge of sharp spines that stretched from its spiked nose to its barbed and stinging tail. It could have been a *Stegasaur* or an *Ankylosaur*.[31]

Saxo Grammaticus, in his work *Gesta Danorum*, relates the plight of the Danish king Frotho and his fight with a giant reptile. A local man had first-hand knowledge of the beast and wanted to help the king get rid of the monster. He described the serpent to the king as:

. . . wreathed in coils, doubled in many a fold, and with a tail drawn out in whorls, shaking his manifold spirals and shedding venom . . . his slaver [saliva] burns up what it bespatters . . . remember to keep the dauntless temper of thy mind; nor let the point of the jagged tooth trouble thee, nor the starkness of the beast, nor the venom . . . there is a place under his lowest belly whither thou mayst plunge the blade . . .[32]

Shields bearing Heraldic Dragons

Using the knowledge of this animal's weakness, the *Volsungassaga* tells of the slaying of **Fafnir** by Sigurd. Because of the creature's armor-like hide, Sigurd dug a pit and waited in it until the monster walked over him on its way to get water. Sigurd was then able to attack the creature's soft underbelly and overcome the beast. From this account, we can assume that this creature walked on all fours with its belly close to the ground.[33]

A 10th century Irishman wrote of his encounter with what sounds like a *Stegosaurus*.[34] Giraldus Cambrensis told of another Irish legend in which Tristan of Lyonesse killed a dragon in the 11th century, and Ireland was declared dragon-free by 1188 A.D.[35]

St. George was reported to have slain his first dragon in Africa. Later, in 1098 A.D., he was said to have slain dragons at Mansfeld in the center of Germany. He was also reported to have killed a dragon in Berkshire, England, and the specific location was later named "Dragon Hill."[36]

In the 13th century in France, a dragon called the **Drac** lived on the Rhone River. One town, Draguignan, was named for the dragon attacks which had occurred. Reportedly, the most severe attacks by the creature were in Beaucaire.

A dragon (often confused with a cunning dragon known as a **Tarsque)** lived on the Isle of St. Marguerite off the coast of France during the Middle Ages.[37] It terrorized an area in the south of France near the town of Nerluc.

The creature was described as:
> hulking rather than sinuous — a small mountain of flesh clad in armor-plated scales and supported on six [?] stout legs.

It was reported to eat animals and people, so the locals kept their distance. Lee Niermann suggests that the description might be of a 20 to 25-foot-long *Ankylosaur*, which had a hulking armored body carried low to the ground, so at a distance it might have looked as if it had six legs. He also suggests that the creature's man-eating escapades might have been exaggerated. **Tarsque**-like dragons are mentioned other places in western literature, but they are never said to have harmed anyone.[38]

A reptile of Bures in Suffolk, England, is described in a Chronicle of 1405:

> Close to the town of Bures, near Sudbury, there has lately appeared, to the great hurt of the countryside, a dragon, vast in body, with a crested head, teeth ike a saw, and a tail extending to an enormous length. Having slaughtered the shepherd of a flock, it devoured many sheep . . . [I]n order to destroy him . . . all the country people around were summoned. But when the dragon saw that he was again to be assailed with arrows, he fled into a marsh or mere and there hid himself among the long reeds, and was no more seen.[39]

A Chronicle which still survives today in the Canterbury Cathedral's library reports that on September 26, 1449, two giant reptiles were seen fighting on the bank of the River Stour. One was black and the other "reddish and spotted." Their struggle entertained the locals for an hour before the black monster retreated to his lair. The place has been known ever since as "Sharpfight Meadow."[40]

In the 1500's, the European textbook written in Latin *Historia Animalium* listed many animals that we would call dinosaurs as still alive, though they were becoming more scarce, like endangered species of today. A well-known naturalist of his time, Ulysses Aldrovandus, recorded an encounter between a peasant, Baptista, and a dragon that fits the description of a 10-foot-long *Tanystropheus* (pictured below). The dragon evidently hissed at the peasant's oxen while walking down the road, so Baptista hit it over the head with his walking stick, killing the creature on May 13, 1572, near Bologna, Italy. The naturalist reportedly gained possession of the dragon's carcass, which he measured, stuffed, and displayed in a museum.[41] It was classified as a **Lindworm** in the 16th century terminology.[42]

In Scandinavia, a dragon was reported to inhabit the area north of Lapland, which was so desolate that it was forced

Tanystropheus

to eat mice.[43a]

In 1608, the naturalist Edward Topsell reported that the dragon of Neidenburg, Germany, poisoned wells by bathing in them.[43b]

German Athanatius Kirchyer examined a dragon killed near Rome and commented on its unusual webbed feet.[43c]

A pamphlet published in August 1614 gives the following report of a dragon living near a village already known as Dragon's Green in St. Leonard's Forest in Sussex, England:

> This serpent (or dragon as some call it) is reputed to be nine feete, or rather more, in length, and shaped almost in the form of an axletree of a cart; a quantitie of thickness in the middest, and somewhat smaller at both endes. The former part, which he shoots forth as a necke, is supposed to be an elle long [3ft-9inches or 114cms]; with a white ring, as it were, of scales about it. The scales along his back seem to be blackish, and so much as is discovered under his bellie, appeareth to be red . . . it is like wise discovered to have large feete, but the eye may be there deceived, for some suppose that serpents have no feete . . . [the dragon] rids away (as we call it) as fast as a man can run. His food [rabbits] is thought to be, for the most part, in a coniewarren, which he much frequents . . . there are likewise upon either side of him discovered two great bunches so big as a large footeball, and (as some thinke) and will in time grow to wings, but God, I hope, will (to defend the poor people in the neighborhood) that he shall be destroyed before he grows to fledge.[44a]

The creature was seen in a 3-4 mile radius, and some of the still-living witnesses were listed in the pamphlet, including John Steele, Christopher Holder, and a certain "widow dwelling near Faygate." One local reportedly had his mastiffs attack the dragon, which promptly killed his dogs, but the person managed to escape with his life. Not everyone was so fortunate. The creature had already reportedly killed a man and a woman by spitting its poisonous venom on them.

The pamphlet tells us that, when the Sussex dragon was unintentionally stumbled upon, it was:

> . . . of countenance very proud and at the sight or hearing of men or cattel will raise his neck upright and seem to listen and looke about, with great arrogancy which is fairly typical of reptilian behavior.[44b]

"A True Relation of a Monstrous Serpent seen at Henham (Essex) on the Mount in Saffron Waldon" is another pamphlet that reported sightings of a large reptile on May 27-28, 1669. The last eyewitness reports of the monster that lived in the woods around Fittleworth in Sussex, England, were as late as 1867. It would run at people hissing and spitting if people stumbled upon it unexpectedly, but it is not reported to have hurt anyone.[45]

The famous American Christian educator, Noah Webster, published his *American Dictionary of the English Language* in 1828, 13 years before the word "dinosaur" was first used. This work defines the noun "dragon" under two separate headings. The first heading for "dragon" defines it as:

> 1. A kind of winged serpent, much celebrated in the romances of the Middle Ages.
>
> 2. A fiery, shooting meteor, or

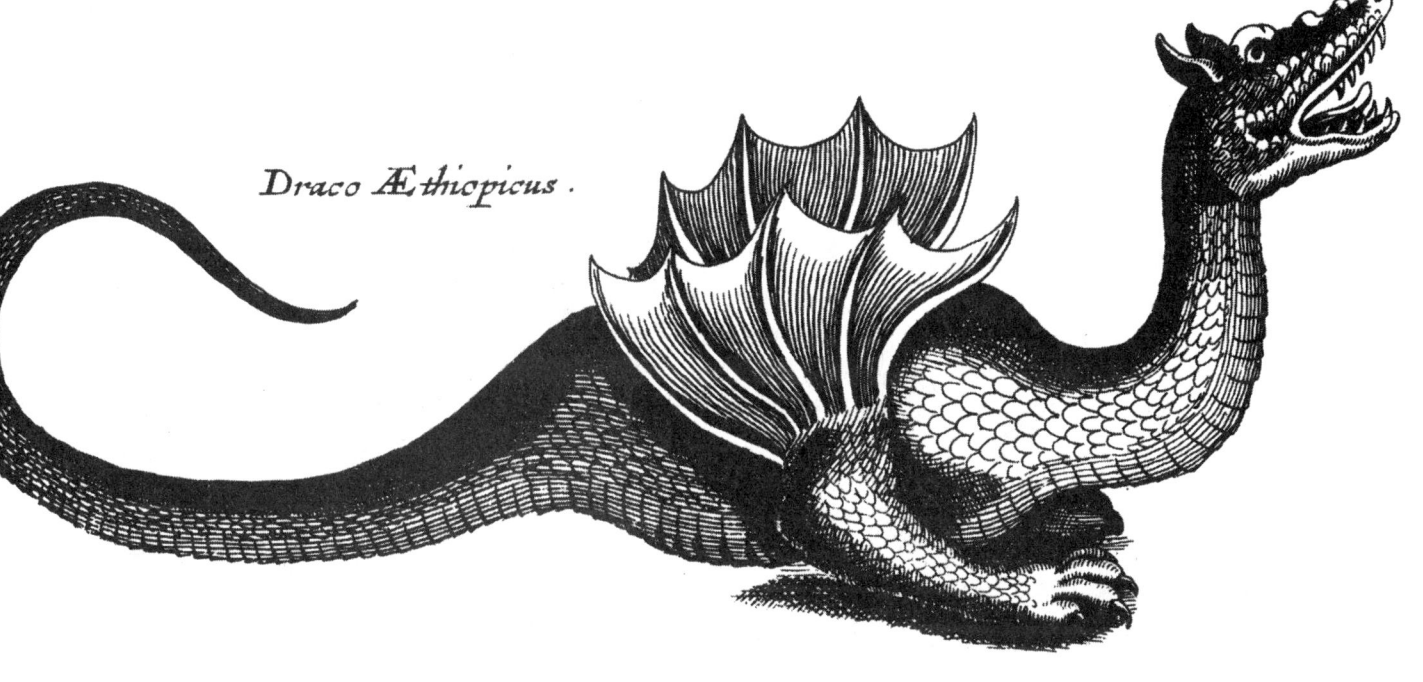

Draco Æthiopicus.

imaginary serpent.

3. A fierce, violent person, male or female; as, this man or woman is a dragon.

4. A constellation of the northern hemisphere.

This dictionary then makes reference to dragons in Scripture as a "large marine fish or serpent" called Leviathan, a "venomous land serpent" as in Psalm 91, and "the devil who is called the old serpent," in the New Testament. Webster's next heading for "dragon" has a single definition:

> A genus of animals, the *Draco*. They have four legs, a cylindrical tail, and membranceous wings, radiated like the fins of a flying-fish.

This is clearly the description of an animal living at the time of the 1828 publication and familiar to people of the early 19th century!

Ivan Sanderson in his book *Investigating the Unexplained* reports that if you look up *Draco* in a Latin-English dictionary, it is a masculine word that means:

> A species of serpent or snake; a dragon (those of the tame sort, especially the Epidaurian, were kept as pets by luxurious Romans).

Once again, a dragon is defined as a living being, not a fairy-tale, and Sanderson is a Naturalist/Evolutionist.

African Dragons

The African wilderness has always been a good place for large animals to flourish. One African reptile attacked the Roman army of General Regulus. According to the Roman historian Livy:

> After many soldiers had been seized in its [the dragon's] mouth, and many more crushed by the folds of its tail, its hide being too thick for javelins and darts, the dragon was at last attacked by military engines and crushed by repeated blows from heavy stones.[46]

The Ethiopian name for dragons was simply "elephant killers."[47] The first-century Roman historian Pliny the Elder described in his *Natural History*:

> Africa produces elephants, but it is India that produces the largest, as well as the dragon, which is perpetually at war with the elephants.[48]

The rock carving in a cave in France (discussed in Chapter 10) of a dinosaur head-butting a mammoth also seems to support the possiblity that dragons and the elephant kind were enemies.

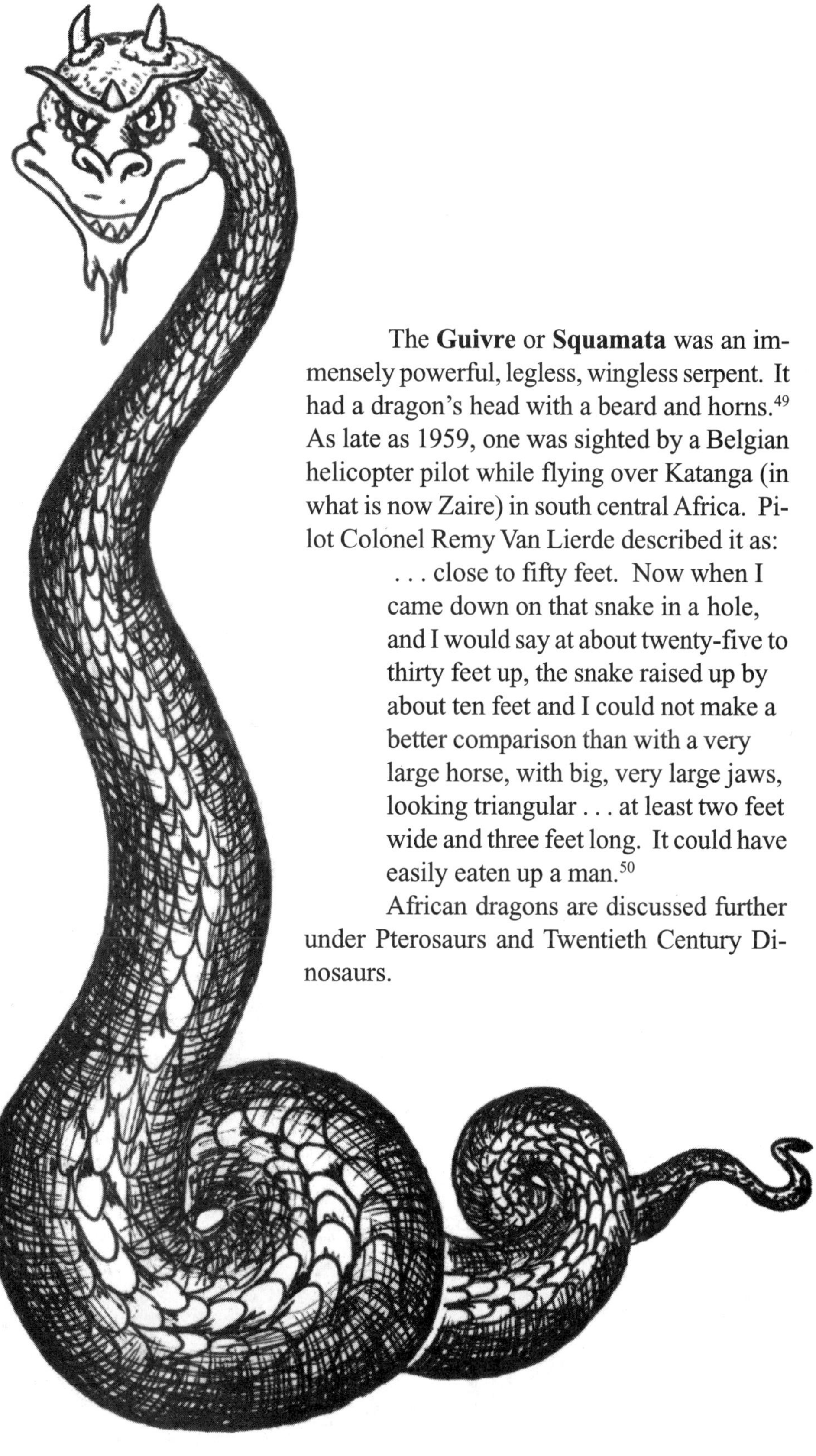

The **Guivre** or **Squamata** was an immensely powerful, legless, wingless serpent. It had a dragon's head with a beard and horns.[49] As late as 1959, one was sighted by a Belgian helicopter pilot while flying over Katanga (in what is now Zaire) in south central Africa. Pilot Colonel Remy Van Lierde described it as:

> . . . close to fifty feet. Now when I came down on that snake in a hole, and I would say at about twenty-five to thirty feet up, the snake raised up by about ten feet and I could not make a better comparison than with a very large horse, with big, very large jaws, looking triangular . . . at least two feet wide and three feet long. It could have easily eaten up a man.[50]

African dragons are discussed further under Pterosaurs and Twentieth Century Dinosaurs.

Australian Dragons

Like much of Africa, the Australian outback has expansive wilderness areas where large reptiles and other wildlife can hide. In 1845 the *Geelong Advisor* newspaper of Victoria, Australia, reported that an unfossilized knee joint from a gigantic animal had been found. It went on to report that when the bone was shown to local Aborigines, they quickly identified it as belonging to a **Bunyip**, which was described as being a frightening monster that walked upright, was amphibious, and laid eggs. These characteristics seem to be a cross between "a bird and an alligator." This creature was even known to have killed some of the native people, and one man named Mumbowran showed, "deep wounds on his breast made by the claws of the animal." A sketch drawn by one Aborigine has the appearance of a bipedal dinosaur.[51]

Australian oral tradition recalls a time when **Kulta** inhabited the swamps and forests that covered inland Australia, now replaced by arid deserts. **Kulta** is described as having a small head on a long narrow neck, a massive, bulky body on four huge legs, and a long pointed tail, which trailed along behind, and sounds suspiciously like a *Sauropod*. The Aborigines' tradition recalls that the "land eventually all dried up, the forests became deserts, the swamps emptied, and **Kulta** died."[52]

This fits the Jehovah's Park scenario. Creatures were reproducing during the post-Flood Ice Age when many areas were receiving more rain than they do now. Rapid climate changes at the end of the Ice Age caused many animals to become extinct, evidently including the Australian *Sauropod* known as **Kulta**.[53]

More recently, cattlemen in the Northern Territory claimed an *Allosaurus*-like beast was mutilating and eating their cattle as late as the 1950's! A tracker, descended from the Australian Aborigines, claimed to have seen an upright-walking reptile 25 feet tall and moving through the brush near Lagoon Creek on the Gulf Coast in 1961.[54]

Geelong Bunyip

Chapter Seven

Flying Dragons

Flying Dragons

Draco alatus Apes ex Greuino Aldro.

The scientific name for a flying reptile is *Pterosaur*, meaning "winged lizard." Many studies of artifacts and written accounts of Egypt and other ancient civilizations depict several different species of *Pterosaurs,* including *Pteranodons, Quetzalcoatlus,* and *Rhamphorhynchus*. There are even variations of *Rhamphorhynchus* described with tail vanes that have not yet been identified in the fossil record.[55] We will explore descriptions of flying dragons from ancient to recent history in this chapter.

Many ancient authors related aerial attacks by cruel venomous flying reptiles. Judging from words used to describe them, they were very agile flyers, which made them hard to avoid when they attacked. The famous Jewish historian Josephus related a historical account of Moses while he was still a prince of Egypt:

> Moses did not march by river, but by land, where he gave a wonderful demonstration of his sagacity; for when the ground was difficult to be passed over, because of the multitude of serpents (which it produced in vast numbers, and indeed is singular in some of those productions, which other countries do not breed, and yet such as are worse than others in power and mischief, and an unusual fierceness of sight, some of which ascend out of the ground unseen, and also ***fly in the air***, and do come upon men at unawares, and do them mischief).
>
> Moses invented a wonderful stratagem to preserve the army safe, and without hurt; for he made baskets like unto arks, of sedge [a grass-like plant], and filled them with ibes [*ibis*], and carried them along with them; which animal is the greatest enemy of serpents imaginable, for they fly from them when they come near them; and as they fly they are caught and devoured by them, as if it were done by the harts [a stag or male deer].
>
> As soon as Moses was to come to the

Figura ex Pareo.

land which was the breeder of these serpents, he let loose the ibes [*ibis*] and by their means repelled the serpentine kind, and used them for his assistance before the army came upon the ground. When he had therefore proceeded thus on his journey, he came upon the Ethiopians before they had expected him; and joining battle with them he beat them.

From this account we see that ibis were a natural predator of small venomous *Pterosaurs*. The Ethiopians apparently depended upon the serpents to stop the passage of people in the serpent-inhabited area; therefore, they did not properly defend that approach. Moses' use of the ibis to overcome the *Pterosaurs* allowed him the advantage of a surprise attack, gaining him the victory.[56]

The Assyrian king Esarhaddon described seeing "yellow serpents that could fly" when he traveled to fight against Tirhaka, king of Egypt and Nubia.[57] Other historians considered reliable who record the existence of flying reptiles are Herodotus, Aelian, Mela, Ammianus, an anonymous 4th century Coptic monk, and 13th century Armenian historian Matthew of Edessa, to name a few.[58]

Aristotle reportedly shot *Rhamphorhynchus* out of the spice trees in Egypt for sport. The winged serpent, called the **Amphitere**, could be found along the banks of the Nile and in Arabia, where they were known to guard frankincense-bearing trees and threatened all who would harvest the precious resin.[59]

The monks of the Monastery of St. Cuthbert were on the island of Lindisfarne, off the east coast of England. In 793 A.D., the monks were disturbed from their prayers and other activities by a mass of hissing sounds likened to "green logs in a bonfire." They found the sky alive with dragons at play: soaring, tumbling, and romping. The monks described how "their scales shimmered in iridescent colors under the weak northern sun."[60]

On November 30, 1222, dragons were seen flying over the city of London. Such migrations preceded thunderstorms and severe flooding. Some people blamed the bad weather on the flying dragons. Others realized that these migrations preceded bad weather, because the creatures were somehow aware of the coming danger and were escaping the threat. Some applied this knowledge as a natural warning system of approaching severe weather.[61]

The **Wyvern** was feared for its viciousness and for the pestilence it brought to northern Europe, Greece, and Ethiopia. It was described as having a coiled trunk and a pair of eagle legs, which were tucked beneath its wings. Its name is derived from the Saxon word "wivere," which meant "serpent." **Wyvern** were apparently *Pterosaurs*.[62]

Martin Luther was evidently familiar with *Ramphorhynchus* in his time. He talked about the tongues at Pentecost being divided like the tails of flying serpents.[63] From the 14th to the 17th centuries there were sightings of many flying dragons in Europe. Renaissance biologists who recorded the flying serpents' existence were Ulysses Aldrovandus of Italy, Konrad Gesner of Switzerland, Edward Topsell of England, and Pierre Belon of France. Belon observed and sketched a flying serpent, which can be identified as a *Rhamphorhynchus*.[64] Naturalist Edward Topsell wrote a report in 1608 describing flying dragons said to plague Santogoarin, Germany; they were even blamed for causing fires.

In 1619, Christopher Schorer, the Prefect of the canton of Solothurn, Switzerland, reported the sightings of winged mountain dragons near Lucerne, Switzerland. A nine-foot-long **Amphitere** lived for several months on a hill near the town of Henham, England, in 1669. Though it terrified many people, it was not reported to have inflicted any real harm.[65]

In 1856, workmen digging a railway tunnel through a mountain in France used gunpowder to move a boulder that was in their way. After the explosion, they pulled a creature from the rubble. It was still alive, but critically injured. It looked like a giant bat, and had a wingspan of over 10 feet. It had black oily skin, a

Wyvern

long neck, and rows of sharp teeth in a beak-like mouth. When they got it out of the tunnel into the light, it started to struggle and then died. After examining the creature, scientists concluded that it was a *Pterosaur*, probably a *Pterodactyl*.[66]

The people of the Sioux Nation called flying dragons **Thunderbirds**, and their image is still seen in the triangular bird-like creatures decorating the sides of many teepees.[67] Native Americans from Alaska to Mexico record legends of gigantic flying monsters.

Colonies of small flying serpents were still a feature of Welsh life until the late 1800's. At the turn of the 20th century, two separate eyewitness descriptions are available. Marie Trevelyan, an elderly Welsh citizen relates:

> The woods round Penllyne Castle, Glamorgan, had the reputation of being frequented by winged serpents, and these were the terror of old and young alike. An aged inhabitant of Penllyne, who died a few years ago [around the turn of the century], said that in his boyhood, the winged serpents were described as very beautiful. They were coiled when in repose, and 'looked as if they were covered with jewels of all sorts. Some of them had crests sparkling with all the colours of the rainbow.' When disturbed, they glided swiftly, 'sparkling all over,' to their hiding places. When angry, they 'flew over people's heads, with outspread wings bright, and sometimes with eyes too, like the feathers in a peacock's tail.' He said it was, 'no old story invented to frighten children,' but a real fact. His father and uncle had killed some of them, for they were 'as bad as foxes for poultry.' The old man attributed the extinction of the winged serpents to the fact that they were 'terrors in the farm yards and coverts.'

An old woman had heard the people of Penmark Place, Glamorgan, Wales, speak of the ravages of the winged serpents in their neighborhood. She related that there was a "king and queen" of the winged serpents in the woods around Bewper, Wales. Her grandfaher and his brother had caught one and a fierce fight had ensued. She too confirmed that they were as notorious "as any fox" in the farmyard and coverts.[68]

Zoologist Ivan Sanderson led an expedition in 1932 to the Cameroons in the Assumbo Mountains in west central Africa. While crossing a river, a large black eagle-sized flying animal doved at him. As he ducked, he noticed that its open mouth was full of pointed teeth. He saw the creature again at dusk and heard it chattering its teeth and swishing its wings as it dove at Sanderson's companion, Gerald. They estimated the creature's wingspan to be at least 12 feet. They described it as flying with a swimming motion and as being coal black with opaque wings. The natives called it **Olitiau**.

Because of Sanderson's Naturalist Spectacles, he believed the animal to be a giant bat of a species yet undiscovered, though he admitted that the creature seemed to look more reptilian than mammalian. Bats are not known to be very aggressive. The creature's teeth were pointed, set apart like a carnivore's teeth and were unlike bat's teeth. Most fish-eating bats are comparatively small, unlike **Olitiau**. The natives were so frightened of the animal that they asked Sanderson and his party to leave. When Sanderson politely explained that they still had work to do in the area, the natives chose to leave.[69]

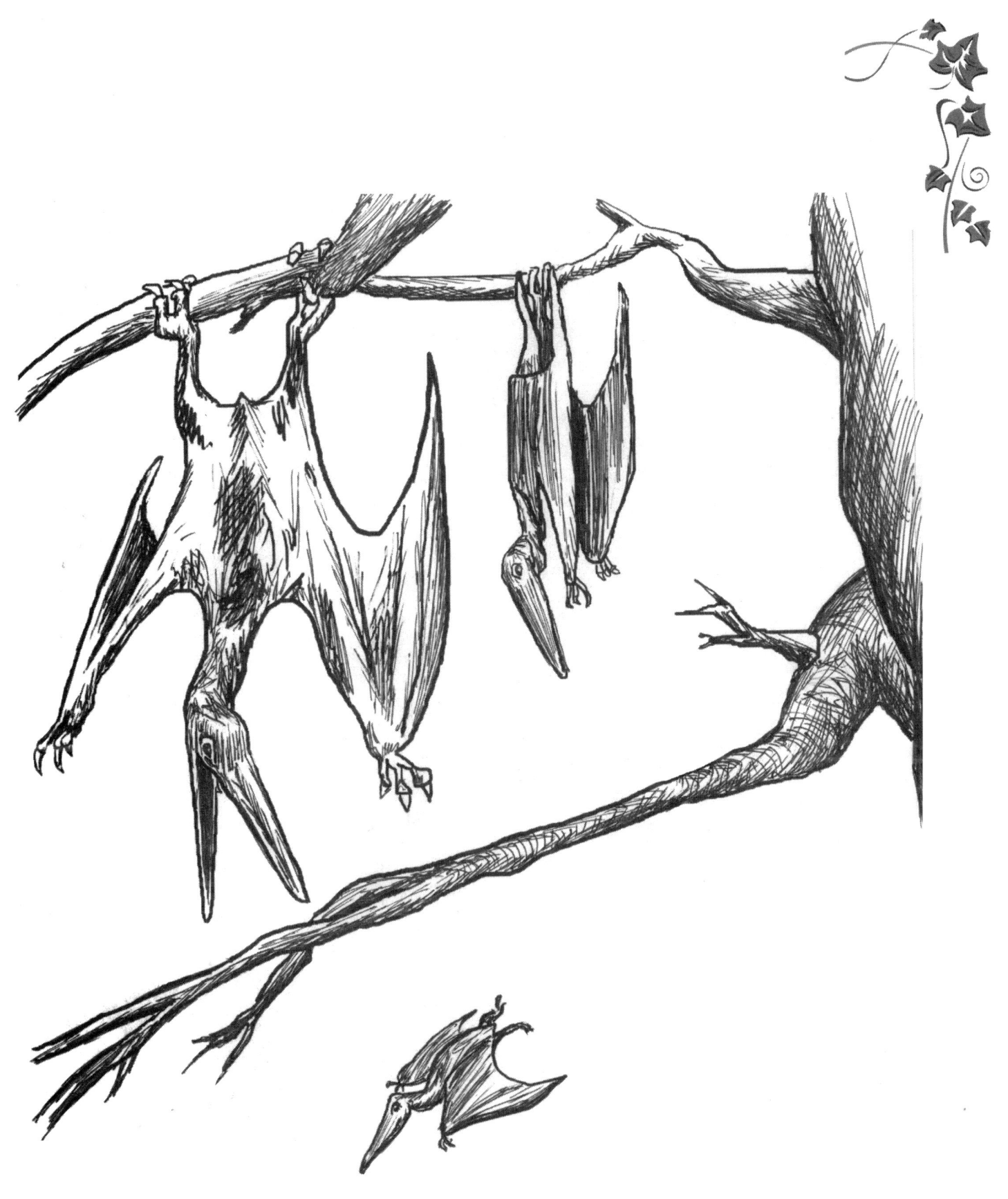

Another flying reptile is described in Frank H. Melland's book *In Witch Bound Africa*, a serious study of the ethnography of Rhodesia. Natives called the creature **Kongomato** and told Melland, "it isn't really a bird; it is more like a lizard with wings like a bat." It was generally a red color, and had a wingspan of 4-7 feet, skin with no feathers, and teeth in its beak. After showing natives numerous pictures of birds and animals, each native unerringly identified the drawing of a *Pterodactyl* as **Kongomato**. They live in the Jiundu swamp, which Melland described as a 50 square-mile swamp of big trees, tangled undergrowth, matted creeping plants, and exotic ferns. According to the natives, **Kongomato** is amphibious, fishing and even swimming very well. This possibly explains its name, which means "overwhelmer of boats," an interesting designation for a flying creature. Just as a point of interest, bats don't swim.[70]

At least two sightings of a huge bird-like creature resembling a reconstruction of a *Pterodactyl* were reported in the 1970's. In the spring of 1974, a Swedish Museum official who wanted to remain unnamed reported that an expedition in Kenya had seen a huge bird-like creature. Another one was sighted the following year in another swampy region in Africa, this time by an American expedition in Namibia.

Chapter Eight

Sea Dragons

Sea Dragons

Dr. Fredrick A. Lucas served as president of the American Museum of Natural History for many years. When asked about sea and lake monsters, he stated, "there is more sworn evidence for the beast than a court of law would need to prove any ordinary case." Stories of giant sea monsters date from the beginnings of written secular history less than 5000 years ago and continue presently. Even the great philosopher Aristotle told of sea serpents attacking and capsizing ships off the coast of Libya.[71]

Within the last century, some dishonest people have tried to benefit from fraudulent reports of sea and lake monster sightings. The following accounts will only be ones considered trustworthy, having withstood the test of time. The many terrifying encounters with giant squids and octopi will not be included, because we are only exploring reports of reptiles, thus staying within our dragon designation.

In 1555, Archbishop Olaus Magnus of Sweden described seeing a sea monster 200 feet long with a circumference of 20 feet. He described this ship-sinking monster as being covered with scales, and having fiery eyes and a lion's mane.[72]

The Danish missionary Hans Egede, known as the apostle of Greenland, was a reputable minister known for his sharp eye for details and intense love of natural history. He reportedly sighted a sea monster on his 1734 voyage to Greenland and gave a remarkable and sober description of the creature he observed:

> The monster was of so huge a size that, coming out of the water, its head reached as high as the mainmast; its

Danish missionary Hans Egede's sea monster sighting in 1734

A committee of the Linnaean Society of New England collected investigative reports describing the animal: it had a multi-humped back, moved by undulating vertically, and held its head 6-12 inches above the water, resembling a snake or turtle. The Linnaean Society mistakenly called this sea serpent a snake, but snakes can't undulate vertically or sink straight down as the creature had been observed to do.[74]

On August 8, 1848, the British ship *HMS Daedalus* was in South Atlantic waters near the Cape of Good Hope. Captain Peter M'Quhae and seven other British officers got a good view of a creature approaching them. The captain reported:

> Its head and shoulders kept about four feet constantly above the surface of the sea. It had no fins but something like a mane of a horse, or rather a bunch of seaweed, washed about its back.[75]

The visible portion alone of the creature measured more than 60 feet in length. It appeared to be only 15 inches in diameter (possibly being the diameter of the creature's neck or tail). It looked dark brown with yellowish white at

body was as bulky as the ship, and three or four times as long. It had a long, pointed snout and spouted like a whale-fish. It had great broad paws; the body seemed covered with shellwork, and the skin was very ragged and uneven. The under part of its body was shaped like an enormous huge serpent, and . . . its tail . . . seemed a whole ship's length distant from the bulkiest part of the body.[73]

During the 17 days from August 6 to 23, 1817, an enormous sea monster was seen "frolicking" in the ocean near Glouster, Massachusetts. On August 14th a group of 20-30 people saw it, including the Glouster Justice of the Peace, Lonson Nash. A ship's carpenter who pursued the creature in a boat described it as a "strange marine animal, resembling a serpent." He further described the monster as smooth-skinned, dark in color with a white throat and belly, and at least 40 feet long with a head the size of a "four gallon keg." It moved vertically "like a caterpillar" and speeded along between 20 and 30 miles per hour.

the throat. It moved at an estimated 12-15 mph with no visible means of propulsion.[76]

William Taylor, captain of the ship *HMS British Banner*, made the following report of his experience with a sea monster:

> On the 25th of April, in lat. 12 deg. 7 min. 8 sec. N., and long. 93 deg. 52 min. E., with the sun over the mainyard, felt a strong sensation as if the ship was trembling. Sent the second mate aloft to see what was up. The latter called out to me to go up the fore rigging and look over the bow. I did so, and saw an enormous serpent shaking the bowsprit with its mouth.
>
> It must have been at least 300 feet long; was about the circumference of a very wide crinoline petticoat, with black back, shaggy mane, horn on the forehead, and large glaring eyes placed rather near the nose, and jaws about eight feet long. He did not observe me, and continued shaking the bowsprit and throwing the sea alongside into a foam until the former came clear away from the ship. The serpent was powerful enough, although the ship was carrying all sail, and going at about ten knots at the time he attacked us, to stop her way completely. . .[77]

The prominent British scientific journal *Nature* published 19 articles on sea serpents between 1872 and 1885. Interest in sea serpents has since waned.[78]

In 1877, a sea monster was sighted off the coast of Sicily by the captain and several officers of a British ship. They described it as having a six-foot-wide head, which came out of the water on a thirty-foot-long neck attached to fifteen-foot-wide shoulders; it was propelled by fifteen-foot-long flippers.[79] This was a large individual!

Naturalists E.G.B. Meade-Waldo and Michael J. Nicoll noticed a six-foot-long "fin or frill" in the waters off Parahiba, Brazil, aboard the yacht *Valhalla* of the Earl of Crawford on December 7, 1905. Through binoculars, they saw a head and neck rise out of

the water; 7-8 feet of it was visible, and it was as big around as "a slight man's body." It was dark brown on top and whitish underneath, and its head and eyes resembled those of a turtle.[80]

Since the advent of powered vessels, ships began adhering more closely to the sea-routes than when wind power was used. The sea serpents are not sighted as frequently anymore, possibly because the creatures know to avoid the sea routes. The noise from engines would serve as a good warning to vacate the area. Because of this, most modern sightings of sea dragons are from shore or small boats in seas or deep-water lakes.

Sea serpent sightings were often ridiculed. One ship's captain refused to look when the officer of the watch summoned him to the bridge to see a sea monster. "Had I said that I had seen the sea serpent," he explained, "I would have been considered a warranted liar all my life."[81] With this kind of social pressure brought to bear on witnesses, many sightings probably went unreported.

The British warship, *HMS Hillary*, was sailing off the coast of Iceland in 1917 when the crew sighted a sea monster. The captain described seeing "a sea monster with a cow-like head on a neck about twenty-eight feet long."[82]

From 1914 to 1919, a sea monster frequented the coast of San Clemente, California. In the warm waters of the Outer Santa Barbara Channel, members of the Tuna Club, America's first big-game fishing club, saw the monster regularly. Descriptions by witnesses were so consistent, one interviewer said, "It was almost as though a recording had been made and each man played the same recording." He added, "These men were all interviewed separately and none of them knew that I had talked to anyone else about the San Clemente monster." The creature was described by the Tuna Club secretary, Ralph Bandini, as being dark in color with a long thick columnar neck, and a mane which looked like fine seaweed or coarse hair. It had enormous protuberant eyes a good 12 inches in diameter, which were horrifying, dull, and lifeless. The neck and head stood 10 feet out of the water and were 5-6 feet in diameter. Similar to the reports of other sea monsters, it sunk straight down. Bandini estimated its size as larger than the largest whale, because the waves didn't move it as much as they moved a whale.[83]

In 1925, the carcass of a sea creature washed up on the beach at Santa Cruz, California. Some believe it was the sea monster called the **Old Man**, which had frequented that area for several years. The animal was reported to have had a 30-foot-long neck, a huge head, and a duck-like beak. E.L. Wallace, president of the National History Society of British Columbia, examined it thoroughly and claimed it had no teeth, a large head, and a 20-foot-long neck. He called it a *Plesiosaur*. Later, other biologists claimed it was the remains of an extremely rare beaked whale from the North Pacific.[84]

In the early 1900's, off the coast of Vancouver Island, Canada, many have reported seeing a sea serpent nicknamed **Caddy**. Judge James Thomas Brown and family of Saskatchewan reported seeing **Caddy** about 150 yards offshore. They reported:

> His head like a snake's came out of the water four or five feet straight up. Six or seven feet from the head, one of his big coils showed clearly. The coil itself was six or seven feet long, fully a foot thick, perfectly round and dark in color . . . It seemed to look at us for a moment and then dived. It must have been swimming very fast for when it came up again, it was about 300 yards away . . . I got three good looks at him. On one occasion he came up right in front of us. There was no question about the serpent – it was quite a sight. I'd think the creature was thirty-five to forty feet long. It was like a monstrous snake. It certainly wasn't any of those sea animals we know, like a porpoise, sea lion, and so on. I've seen them and know what they look like.[85]

On the morning of February 4, 1934, Cyril Andrews and Norman Georgeson were out duck hunting off the rocky shore of South Pender Island, Vancouver, Canada. After badly wounding one duck, they paddled their boat out to retrieve it. When they neared the bird, they saw "a head and two loops or segments" of something moving toward the wounded duck. From only about 10 feet away, the mesmerized men watched as it opened its mouth and gulped down the duck and then proceeded to snap at a few sea gulls before disappearing into the water. They said it was grayish-brown and had saw-like teeth and a pointed tongue in its horse-shaped head. Andrews rushed to shore to phone Justice of the Peace G.F. Parkyn of Bedwell Harbor, who arrived with several others in time to see the monster's body undulating rhythmically and its head apparently resting on the surface of the water about 20 yards offshore. Andrews estimated the creature to have been about 40 feet long and 2-3 feet in diameter at its thickest point, with a three-foot-long head.[86]

In WWI a German submarine captain filed the following report:

> On July 30, 1915, our U28 torpedoed the British steamer *Iberian* carrying a rich cargo in the North Atlantic. The steamer sank quickly, the bow sticking almost vertically into the air. When it had gone for about twenty-five seconds there was a violent explosion. A little later pieces of wreckage, and among them a gigantic sea animal (writhing and struggling wildly), was

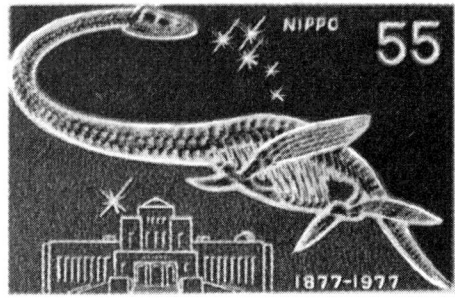

Commemorative Japanese stamp of a *Plesiosaur*

shot out of the water to a height of 60-100 feet. At that moment I had with me in the conning tower my officers of the watch, the chief engineer, the navigator, and the helmsman. Simultaneously, we all drew one another's attention to this wonder of the seas . . . we were unable to identify it. We did not have the time to take a photograph, for the animal sank out of sight after ten or fifteen seconds. It was about 60 feet long, was like a crocodile in shape, and had four limbs with powerful webbed feet and a long tail tapering to a point.[87]

This could be a description of a *Kronosaurus*.

In January of 1950, after a three-day gale, a hulking 40-foot-long carcass with huge walrus-like tusks washed up on the beach in Ataka, Egypt, in the Gulf of Suez. The creature was never positively identified.[88]

On April 10, 1977, the Japanese fishing vessel *Zuiyo Maru*, was trawling off the coast of Christchurch, New Zealand, when it caught a 4000-pound carcass in its nets at a depth of 900 feet. The crew pulled up a dead 32-foot-long animal with a long neck and tail, and four flippers. The corpse was in such a decayed, foul-smelling state, that it was thrown back into the sea after measurements and photographs were taken. Japanese paleontologists concluded that it probably was a *Plesiosaur* after studying photographs and sketches drawn by fishing company executive Michihiko Yano. To commemorate the find, the Japanese made a *Plesiosaur* postage stamp. Currently, scientists claim that the creature was just the rotting remains of a basking shark. Without the actual remains, the identity of the carcass cannot be known for sure. However, there have been so many sightings of sea monsters that this one is really not worth arguing about.[89]

Sea monsters have been seen all over the world. The sightings have become less frequent, but logically so, since ships have been equipped with noisy engines and follow sea routes more closely.

Carcass of a sea creature that was believed, by some, to be the remains of a *Plesiosaur*.

Water Monster?

Chapter Nine

Lake Dragons

Lake Dragons

With our Biblical Spectacles on, we see that the Floodwaters of The Genesis Flood receded about 4400 years ago. (See Parts 6 and 7 in Appendix B.) As sea levels dropped, lakes and other inland bodies of water were formed all over the world. Marine creatures passing through these deep-water areas would have been trapped in inland water. Some lake monsters could have survived, and their descendants could have populated inland waters for hundreds and even thousands of years. However, eventually, most of them did disappear.

Europe

Scotland's monstrous reptiles of the lochs (lakes in Scotland) have been sighted since the Dark Ages. The most famous lake monster has to be the Loch Ness monster, often called **Nessie**. In ancient times, local residents used to sacrifice animals to the creature that lived in the loch. In 565 A.D., the Irish missionary Saint Columba visited Loch Ness as told in *The Life of St. Columba* by Adamnan. The lake monster had mauled and killed a local man. One of St. Columba's servants, Lugne, swam across the narrows at the head of the loch to retrieve a small boat they had left behind. While swimming back, he came face to face with "a very odd-looking beastie, something like a huge frog, only it was not a frog." The monster started to attack Lugne but was stopped by the missionary's rebuke, "Go thou no further nor touch the man. Go back at once!" As reported in the biography, "the monster was terrified and fled away again more quickly than if it had been dragged on by ropes . . ." Many on-lookers were so taken by St. Columba's power that many were converted to Christian-

St. Columba rebuking one of the Loch Ness monsters in 565 A.D.

ity on the spot. (One hypothesis is that the creature might have been defending its young, thus explaining its aggressive behavior.)

St. Columba was said to have done such a good job of rebuking the creature that no one reported seeing it again until the 1800's. When it was spotted again, children were not allowed to play near the loch for fear of the beast. Since the late 1880's, there have been over 4000 sightings of Nessie. Ninety percent of these sightings have occurred when the water is still and calm.[90]

In 1933, a highway was built along the

shore of the loch, and the number of sightings skyrocketed, probably due to the greatly increased number of people along the shore. Over 1000 sightings have been reported since WWII alone.

In 17 of those sightings, **Nessie** was out of the water moving something like a seal on its flippers. While enjoying a Scottish vacation, a London businessman and his wife, Mr. and Mrs. George Spicer, saw an enormous, long-necked animal emerge out of the bracken onto the road on the afternoon of July 22, 1933. It moved its hulking body across the road in a jerking action and disappeared into the brush on the loch side. They recalled that the monster's neck undulated "in the manner of a scenic railway." They said it was a "terrible dark elephant grey, of a loathsome texture, reminiscent of a snail."[91]

The following winter, another sighting was reported. At about 1:00 a.m. on a moonlit night in January of 1934, medical student Arthur Grant was riding his motorcycle along the loch road when he noticed a large dark blob on the side of the road ahead. When he drew near, "the blob" bounded across the road, almost colliding with him! He described the jaywalker as a creature with a small eel-like head, oval eyes, a long neck, a bulky body thickening toward a long rounded-off tail, and four flipper-like legs. He thought it was about 18-20 feet long and had dark whale-like skin. Grant bravely (or foolishly) got off his motorcycle and chased the creature down to the loch where he watched it disappear into the dark, cold water. Grant said, "it looked like a hybrid – a cross between a *Plesiosaur* and a member of the seal family."[92]

On October 8, 1936, **Nessie** entertained residents, two tour buses, and several carloads of people for a full 15 minutes. About 50 people, many armed with telescopes and binoculars, excitedly watched the monster's peaceful passage across the still loch waters until it suddenly disappeared. All described it as something with two humps behind a head and neck.[93]

Enough information exists on **Nessie** that whole books are written just on the creatures of Loch Ness. But before we desert the Loch Ness saga, there is one more point of interest to be covered. In 1972, an expedition of the Academy of Applied Science led by Dr. Robert H. Rines successfully got a picture of the beastie's fin. They used advanced sonar equipment and a camera strobe light system developed for underwater photography by Dr. Edgerton of MIT. The visibility of the water in Loch Ness is extremely limited because vegetation from the steep mountainsides surrounding the loch is constantly being washed into the water. This fact has hampered many other scientific efforts to find **Nessie**. To increase the chance of photographing **Nessie**, the team of scientists set up automatic cameras to take a series of photographs, 45 seconds apart. On

An underwater photograph of Nessie's fin was taken by Dr. Robert H. Rines of the Academy of Applied Science.

the night of August 8, 1972, they successfully photographed a 4 to 6-foot-long diamond-shaped flipper in motion. A third picture is believed to show two large objects swimming about 12 feet apart.[94]

In 1893, Dr. Farquhar Matheson and his wife sighted a loch monster while sailing on Loch Alsh in Scotland. He later wrote describing the monster:

> It was brown in color, shining and with a sort of ruffle at the junction of its head and neck . . . It moved its head from side to side, and I saw the reflection of the light from its wet skin . . . I saw no body —only the ripple of the water where the line of the body should be. I should judge, however, that there must have been a large base of body to support such a neck. It was . . . of the nature of a gigantic lizard, I should think. An eel could not lift up its body like that.[95]

Morag, the monster of Loch Morar, the deepest lake in Great Britain, twenty miles from Loch Ness, was first sighted in 1895. A song was written about it:

> **Morag**, harbinger of the deep
> Giant swimmer in the deep-green Morar
> The loch which has no bottom
> There it is **Morag** the monster lives.

In 1969, two fishermen had a personal encounter with **Morag** when it rammed their fishing boat. One of the fishermen tried to beat it off with an oar, which snapped in half when it struck the creature. Duncan McDonnell, one of the fishermen, said:

> Its skin was like that of an eel, only rougher in texture. I do not believe it came to attack us and I do not believe it is a monster. I believe it is some sort of overgrown eel.[96]

British biologist Dr. Neil Bass saw a "black, smooth-looking, hump-shaped object" in the loch on July 14, 1970. In August, zoology student Alan Butterworth sighted **Morag** through his binoculars. He described it as having a "dark colored hump, shaped like a dome and looked like a rocky inlet." There have been at least 40 sightings of **Morag** since WWII. Sightings have also been reported in Loch Lomond, Loch Awe, and Loch Rannoch.

In 1860, an English clergyman and author, Sabine Baring-Gould, wrote of the **Skrimsl** of Ireland, which was reported to be 50 feet long and looked something like **Nessie**. Baring-Gould wrote:

> I should have been inclined to set the whole story down as myth, were it not for the fact that the accounts of all the witnesses tallied with remarkable minuteness, and the monster is said to have been seen not in one portion of the lake (the Lagarflot) only, but at different points.

He also wrote of a slimy gray-brown creature seen in Lake Suldal in Norway; its head and neck were said to be as big as a rowboat. There was a story that the monster had grabbed one man's arm when he was crossing the lake in a small boat. He was released after reciting the Lord's Prayer, but the arm was badly mangled and never able to be used again.[97]

Several sightings of a lake monster have been made in lake Lough Fadda, Ireland. In 1954, Mrs. Georgina Carberry saw "a black object which moved slowly, showing two humps" while fishing with friends. Pat Walsh saw the animal's head and neck emerge, and a family of seven described it as a "black animal about twelve feet long." A local shepherd even

reported seeing it on shore near the lake.[98]

In the 18th century, a man in Wales was swimming in a lake and "before anyone could render aid the man was enveloped in the coils of the monster . . ." Apparently, the man's body was never recovered.[99]

Two mountain climbers were climbing the mountain beside a deep lake in Glaslyn (Snowdon), Wales, when they looked down into the lake and saw the **Afancs**. They described it as having a long gray body, rising from the depths of the lake to the surface where it raised its head, looked around, and then resubmerged.

In 1765, *The Gentleman's Magazine* of London carried an article reading;
> The people of Stockholm report that a great dragon, named **Necker**, infests the neighboring lake, and seizes and devours such boys as go into the water to wash.

The Bishop of Avranches wanted to test the truth of the article and took a swim in Lake Malaren one sunny day, and onlookers said they "were greatly surprised when they saw him return from imminent danger."[100]

Sweden also had a lake monster. On the island of Forso, in Lake Storsjon near Ostersund, a sketch of the beast can be seen on an old stone. The creature is depicted with flippers and a long neck. The period of the creature's greatest activity was reported between 1820 and 1898. The Lake Storsjon monster is described as looking like a large reddish-colored sea horse with a white mane. This creature has been estimated to move at an incredible 45 mph. In 1946, three people described the surface of the lake to be "broken by a giant snakelike object with three prickly, dark humps. It swam at a good parallel to the shore, on which the waves caused by the object were breaking." Additional sightings were reported in 1965.[101]

Asia

Lake Monsters have been reported throughout Russia and China. In 1964, scientists from Moscow University were on an expedition surveying mineral deposits in eastern Siberia. They decided to explore Lake Khaiyr looking for the monster rumored to live there. The lake is near the Laptevykill Sea in the region of Yakutia in Siberia. Team biologist, N. Gladkikh went to the lake to draw water and saw a creature that had crawled on shore. His report stated:

> The animal had a small head, long, gleaming neck, a huge body covered with a jet black skin, and a vertical fin along the spine.

The next time the creature was seen, deputy leader of the team G. Rokosuev was with Gladkikh, removing any doubts about the biologist's credibility. Rokosuev wrote:

> Suddenly a head appeared in the center of the lake, then a dorsal fin. The creature beat the water with its long tail, producing waves on the lake. You can imagine our astonishment when we saw with our own eyes that the stories were true. That the lake is inhabited by a monster has long been known to the local population. Nobody would approach the lake because of it.

Gladkikh sketched the creature after having seen it on land and in the water. The story and sketches were published in a Russian newspaper in 1964.[102]

Two official Chinese newspapers reported **USO's (Unidentified Swimming Objects)** sighted in lakes in Manchuria and Tibet during 1980. The *Peking Evening News* reported that a strange creature resembling a dinosaur had been spotted numerous times in Wenbu Lake in a remote region of Tibet. It was even reported to have seized a yak that had unwisely paused to graze near the

Gladkikh's sketch of the Lake Khaiyr monster

lakeshore. The man taking the yak to market who reported the event was the local Communist Party Official. Other sightings were made at a crater lake near a mountain peak in the Jilin Province, according to the same newspaper. Visitors and staff members of a nearby weather station described the creature's head as being shaped similar to a cow's head but much larger, with a flat duck-like beak. They also reported that it swam quickly enough to cause a wake like a motorboat.

In late 1980, the *Guangming Daily* reported the sightings of a lake creature in the Changbai mountain region of Manchuria. The respected Chinese author Lei Jia twice saw a black reptile about two yards long with a long neck and oval head. Three local weather bureau officials confirmed the creature's existence when they saw and shot at the beast. But to the creature's joy and their dismay, they missed, and then it wisely disappeared. The Chinese used to worship dragons, so their action might have confused the beastie.[103]

United States of America

The most famous lake monster in the USA is **Champ**, named by the chamber of commerce in Port Henry, New York. **Champ** inhabits Lake Champlain, a very long thin lake that reaches 700 feet deep in places and stretches along the border between New York and Vermont. Lake Champlain used to be an arm of the sea, as the lochs in Scotland once were. The French explorer for whom the lake is named, Samuel de Champlain, reported seeing a creature about 20 feet long, as thick as a barrel with a horse-shaped head: "A great long monster, lying in the lake, allowing birds to land on its back, then snapping them in whole."

Since then, more than 100 sightings have been reported, including five in 1980.[104]

One photograph taken of **Champ** showed a creature with a long neck, humped back, and flippers. The picture was tested for fraud at the Kitt Peak National Observatory near Tuscon, Arizona. The results showed the picture had not been faked and that the object was surfacing, not just bobbing or floating. Sandy Manci's photograph of **Champ** appears on the cover of the book *Champ – Beyond the Legend*. Lee Smith had been videotaping the lake when he was blessed to catch a glimpse of **Champ** on tape. There are evidently many residents of the area who have seen the creature, but don't want to admit they saw it because they fear what people might think. The town fathers of Port Henry, New York, passed an official resolution on October 6, 1980, forbidding anyone from harassing **Champ**.[105]

A lesser-known lake monster was sighted in Bear Lake, Utah. For many years the Native Americans had seen it and called it the **Beast of the Storm Spirits**. Local settlers did not take reports of the creature seriously until a respected local citizen reported seeing it while riding along the eastern shoreline on July 27, 1860. The next day, four other people saw the monster and reported that it was moving and swam "much faster than a horse could run on land." The **Bear Lake Monster** was sighted for many decades afterward.[106]

The first reported sighting of the **White River Monster** of Arkansas was in 1937 in the area of Newport. Plantation owner Bramlett Bateman claimed to have seen the creature several times. Seeing it at a distance, he described it as "about 12 feet long and 5 feet wide." He could see neither the creature's head nor its tail.

Champ

Zuglodon

Many sightings have been made since then.

On July 28, 1971, Cloyce Warren of the White River Lumber Company went fishing on the river with two friends when they were startled by a column of water spewing into the air about 200 feet away. Warren told reporters later:

> This giant form rose to the surface and began moving in the middle of the river, away from the boat. It was very long and gray colored . . . I grabbed a camera [he had brought it to photograph their catch] and managed to get a picture right before it submerged. It appeared to have a spiny backbone that stretched for 30 or more feet. It was hard to make out exactly what the front portion looked like, but it was awfully large.[107]

Creation Evangelist Kent Hovind hypothesizes from the existing testimonies that it might have been a *Zuglodon* or *Baskolasaurus*. In February 1973, the Arkansas State Senate passed a bill to protect the **White River Monster**, establishing the **White River Monster** Sanctuary and Refuge. Sadly, the last reported sighting was in 1972.

In 1941, sightings of a lake monster started to be reported in Lake Payette, Idaho. It was called **Slimy Slim**. During July and August of that year, over 30 people boating on the lake saw it, to their utter amazement. Thomas L. Rogers, the city attorney of Boise, told reporters:

> The serpent is about fifty feet long and going five miles per hour with a sort of undulating movement . . . His head, resembled that of a snub-nosed crocodile, was eight inches above the water. I'd say he was about thirty-five feet long, on consideration.

Thirty people have reported seeing the Chesapeake Bay monster, nicknamed **Chessie**. In the summer of 1978, it was sighted in the Potomac River about sixty miles northeast of Richmond, Virginia. John Merriner, a fishery scientist from Virginia Institute of Marine Science, believes **Chessie** is a large tropical snake, probably a type of anaconda.[108]

In the USA, there have been sightings of lake or sea monsters in about half of the states. Among them are Alaska's **Lake Iliamna Monster, Bessie** the Lake Erie monster, and others too numerous to record here.

Ogopogo

Canada

Many lake monsters have been sighted in Canada. The most famous is British Columbia's **Ogopogo**, or **Naitaka** as the Native Canadians call it. Okanagan Lake, connected to the Pacific Ocean by the Okanagan River and Columbia River, is its home. There have been over, 200 sightings of the creature since the 1700's. In 1854, a Native Canadian reported that he struggled successfully for his life against the monster, although his team of horses wasn't as fortunate; they were pulled under and drowned. A pioneer John McDougal lost his horses to the **Ogopogo**, also.[109]

In the early 20th century, a captain of the Canadian Fishery Patrol saw and described the monster as "a telegraph pole with a sheep's head." An American who saw it said he was struck dumb with terror. On July 2, 1919, the Watson family of Montreal and their friend Mr. Kray reportedly saw **Ogopogo** and described it as:

> a long sinuous body, thirty feet in length, consisting of about five undulations, apparently separated from each other by about a two-foot space . . . The length of each of the undulations . . . would have been about five feet. There appeared to be a forked tail, of which only one-half came above the water.[110]

By the 1920's, **Ogopogo** was so famous that a song was written about it:

> His mother was an earwig
> His father was a whale
> A little bit of head
> And hardly any tail
> And **Ogopogo** was his name.[111]

R.H. Millar, the owner-publisher of a newspaper, saw **Ogopogo** on July 20, 1959, and observed that it was moving at about 15-17 mph. He said, "His head was about 9 inches above the water . . . [and] is definitely snakelike with a blunt nose." He saw 5 humps exposed above the water before it gradually submerged, moving in a smooth graceful motion. It was a dark greenish color, and it tail wasn't visible to them. Four teenage young-men saw something in February of 1977 and described it as having three black humplike protrusions and as making a sizable wake.[112]

Other Canadian lake monsters include **Manipogo** of Winnipeg Lake, which is said to have a roar like a train-whistle, **Igopogo** the dog-faced monster of Simcoe Lake north of Toronto, **T-Zum-A** in Shuswap Lake, British Columbia, and **Hapyxelor** in Muskrat Lake, north of Ottawa.[113]

The sketch drawn of the **Yarru** at a missionary's request appears to be that of a *Plesiosaur*.

Australia

There are many reports of lake monsters in the "Land Down Under." Some of the most interesting reports are about strange disappearances due to a monster that apparently inhabits Lake Galilee in the far western part of Queensland. Livestock that drank from the lake's edge have vanished; fishing boats have been found smashed and the fishermen gone.

Large dark shapes have been reported moving through the lake water. This lake is in remote, thick mountainous bush country and is therefore not well-known. Aborigines would not live on the lake's shore because they feared that the **Bunyip**, which lived in it, would grab anyone foolish enough to canoe in the lake or to wade in its shallows. Oral tradition describes the monster as 20-30 feet long with two pairs of flippers, a long eel-like tail, and a long serpentine neck attached to a bulky body. [114]

In the far north of Queensland, the Kuku Yalanji tribesmen tell of the **Yarru**, which in early times inhabited their water holes. The animal is remembered as having devoured at least one maiden. The sketch drawn of the **Yarru** at a missionary's request appears to be that of a *Plesiosaur*. Near Sydney, the Dharuk people maintain that a huge creature, known as **Mirreeulla**, is still sighted in the Hawkesbury River, although less frequently now, thank God. The monster has been estimated to be up to 50 feet long. [115]

Africa

In 1913, the German government sent a special expedition led by Captain Freiherr von Stein to the Cameroons in Africa to map the territory. He wrote of a mysterious beast which had been described by the local people as:

> brownish gray in color with a smooth skin, its size approximately that of an elephant . . . It is said to have a long flexible neck and only one tooth, but a very long one: some say it is a horn. A few spoke about a long muscular tail like that of an alligator. [116]

World-respected naturalist Ivan T. Sanderson, was on a canoe trip on the Mainyu River in western Africa in 1913. While exploring the river, something astonishing happened. Sanderson wrote:

> The most terrible noise I have ever heard, short of an oncoming earthquake or the explosion of an aerial torpedo at close range, suddenly burst forth from one of the big caves on my right. Something enormous rose out of the water . . This "thing" was shiny black and was the head of something, shaped like a seal but flattened from above to below.

Later, natives told him he had seen **M'koo**. Sanderson said the existence of this creature explained why there were no hippos or crocodiles in the Mainyu River, while there were hundreds of them in two nearby rivers. [117]

Stegosaurus

Chapter Ten

Dinosaurs Recorded in Art

Dinosaurs Recorded in Art

If man lived alongside dinosaurs, as the Bible and history suggest, then we would expect to find dinosaurs recorded in the past, and we do. Chapters 6-9 presented many examples of written reports of dragon sightings. This chapter will present a very small sampling of the images of these creatures that have been recorded in the visual arts.

Creation magazine is an excellent ongoing source about dinosaurs and other topics from the Biblical Creation perspective. Dennis Swift wrote an interesting article, "Messages on Stone – Ancient Rock Art Challenges Evolutionary Theory," which appeared in the March-May 1997 issue. This article includes Pastor Swift's photographs of Inca or pre-Inca engravings on polished rock of a *Triceratops* and an *Allosaur* with spines down its back (possibly a *Spinosaurus* or an *Acrocanthosaurus*). These decorative stones were found on the Nasca Desert Plains in Peru. Some age tests have been done and these pieces are probably not forgeries.

Within 100 yards of an Anasazi Native American ruin in Natural Bridges National Park, there is a petroglyph (an ancient carved rock drawing) of a *Sauropod*. Even the leading regional experts on rock art admit that this petroglyph shows signs of weathering, is authentically old, and is definitely of a *Sauropod*; but being evolutionists, they offer no explanation for its existence.

Similarly, there is a well-weathered petroglyph chiseled into the walls of Havasupal Canyon in Arizona that greatly resembles a bipedal dinosaur balancing on its tail. It also shows signs of true age. Lichen growth has been found in the carved area of the petroglyph, which can be used to date the carving. Lichen can take hundreds and even thousands of years to reach their final size, and so the maturity of the lichen in the carving allows the scientists to estimate how long ago the lichen started to grow, giving a minimum estimated age.

In the American southwest there is a pictograph (picture symbol) of a *Pterosaur* with a prominent crest and long tail. Interestingly, researchers from the University of Ohio quarried a fossil *Pterosaur* not far from this pictograph.

Dr. Carl Baugh of Creation Evidences Museum obtained a polished Mexican petroglyph of a *Pterosaur*. In the photograph, the piece is being held by the emerging young creation scientist and my dear friend Peter DeRosa. The DeRosas offer interested individuals the opportunity to experience dinosaur digs for themselves through Creation Expeditions, Inc. (For more information, please refer to Appendix H.)

Peter DeRosa of Creation Expeditions, Inc. holding a polished Mexican petroglyph.

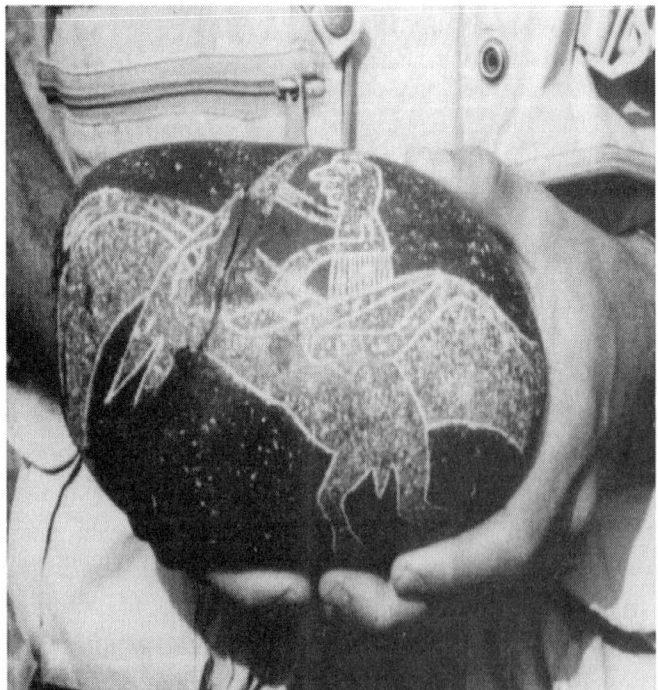

Petroglyph of a *Pterosaur* being ridden by a Native American.

Bernifal Cave carving of a dinosaur head-butting a mammoth

The Ice Age tribe, commonly known as Neanderthals, had a very artistic culture. Their stylized art depicts the animals, which were part of their daily life. Decorating the wall of Bernifal Cave, one Neanderthal dwelling in France, a dinosaur is seen head-butting a mammoth. (This supports the report of Pliny the Elder that dragons and elephants were adversaries.) The artists must have been familiar with these animals, as well as the antelope and other animals included in their work. A photograph of this carving graces Jack Cuozzo's very interesting book *Buried Alive*. The book presents his primary research on the creationist view of Neanderthal man.

There are numerous other examples of dinosaurs in early art. Some of the art is stylized, as in the case of Chinese dragons. Other examples more closely resemble the actual animals to the extent that it is frequently possible to identify what type of creature is depicted. An excellent example is the Roman mosaic picturing two sea monsters, probably *Elasmosaurs*.

Roman Mosaic from the 2nd century A.D.

Bill Cooper's article in *Creation Ex Nihilo Technical Journal Volume 6 (1)* called "The Early History of Man - Part 4: Living Dinosaurs from Anglo-Saxon and Other Early Records" gives many examples of dinosaurs in art. The 8th century Irish Book of Kells depicts anatomically correct images of fish, cats, dogs, and birds, which are easily recognizable. Alongside these are seen creatures which are unrecognizable to us, probably because they are extinct and no longer familiar to us.

An ancient Celtic manuscript, MS 18 at the Amiens Municipal Library, contains a drawing of a man examining the dead body of what appears to be a sea serpent, and I don't mean a sea snake! On a Saxon shield, there is a portrayal of a flying serpent with its wings folded down along its sides. It looks similar to modern reconstructions of *Pterodactyls* made from the fossil record.

Pterodactyl with its wings folded down as portrayed on a Saxon shield

Man examining a dead sea serpent as seen in the Celtic manuscript MS 18 of Amiens Municipal Library.

A large frieze is preserved in the church of Saints Mary and Hardulph at Breedon-on-the-hill in Leicestershire, Great Britain. Along with easily recognizable varieties of birds, plants, and people, there is a graphic portrayal of a bipedal predatory dragon (*Theropod*) attacking a herd of long-necked, four-legged dragons (*Sauropods*). The attacking dragon is depicted as having what appears to be armor plating on its hide. Interestingly, this same description of **Grendel** is found in the Beowulf account. How did early Saxons know the details necessary to accurately portray a *Theropod* if they had never seen one?

A church in Llanbadarn-y-Garrag, Powys, Wales contains a carving of a local giant reptile. It includes large paddle-like flippers, a long neck, and a small head looking very much like a *Plesiosaur*.[118]

Remember in the Beowulf account that the juvenile male **Grendel** was thwarted by Beowulf when he twisted off its small, clawed forelimb. This idea was evidently not a new

one. A man grasping and preparing to amputate the forelimb of a bipedal dragon is found on an extremely early Babylonian cylinder seal. [119]

A nineteenth-century engraving depicts the first 'serpent' reported by Europeans in the New World. It was sighted in the waters off Cape Ann, Massachusetts, in 1639. The monster was reported to have slithered on shore and coiled itself.

Woodcuts from the Middle Ages include interesting interactions between men and dragons. Those included here were in books printed between 1475 and 1500. They have not been redrawn by modern artists. These pictures come from the Dover Pictorial Archives Series and were selected from various volumes of *Der Bilderschmuck der Frühdrucke*, by Albert Schramm.

There are many more examples of dinosaurs in art before 1800. These artists did not have the benefit of museum reconstructions, TV specials, or Hollywood movies to inspire them. They most likely depicted familiar scenes from their daily lives, as seen in their art.

Ancient Babylonian cylinder seal depicting a man preparing to amputate the forelimb of a bipedal dragon

Woodcuts from the Middle Ages of interactions between men and dragons.

Man feeding dragon (oops)

A Knight fighting a bear and a dragon

St. George slaying a dragon

Man killing a dragon

Brontosaurus

Chapter Eleven

Twentieth Century Dinosaurs?!

Twentieth Century Dinosaurs?!

In the early part of the twentieth century, British author Sir Arthur Conan Doyle wrote the mysterious book *The Lost World*. It tells of a hidden land where dinosaurs and other rowdy reptiles still romped and roamed. Many other stories have carried the same theme, including the movie *Baby . . . Secret of the Lost Legend* and more recently the genetically engineered, manmade re-creation of the lost world in the *Jurassic Park* series. Our curiosity about these huge reptiles is often overwhelming. It would be beyond many scientists' wildest hopes or dreams to find a living dinosaur as pictured in the first *Jurassic Park* movie.

Believe it or not, there may be a few dinosaurs still living today! According to historical accounts, they wouldn't cohabit with people very well. So it is no wonder that the recent sightings we hear of are located in the deepest, darkest, most remote jungles and the largest, wettest, most mosquito- and snake-infested swamps still in existence. Did you know that in the Congolese rainforest in the People's Republic of the Congo, there is a swamp the size of the state of Alabama called the Likouala Swamp? This huge swamp is the home of an animal the natives call **Mokele-mbembe**. Much can be learned about this swamp creature through interviewing those who have seen it. From eyewitness accounts, the animal is described as a reddish-brown color below the water. Above the water, it has a 6 to 8-foot-long snake-like head; one man said it had a frill on the top of its head, like the comb of a rooster. It was likened to the size of 5 elephants and

The Congo's *Sauropod* Mokele-mbembe

has clawed feet that make footprints the size of frying pans with three toes.

Mokele-mbembe are known to migrate through the swamp looking for their favorite food, the landolphia fruit, and to dig cave-like hideaways in the riverbanks. Natives that say, to see **Mokele-mbembe** one must quietly look for an area with plenty of landolphia fruit and no hippos, because when **Mokele-mbembe** moves in, the competition moves out. It has been seen rearing up on its hind-legs and planting its forelegs on the bank as it reached for its "jungle-chocolate," as some refer to its favored plant. It has been known to attack canoes when they got too close, killing everyone aboard. But in general, they are thought to have excellent hearing and are considered very shy.

Many scientists have searched for this living dinosaur, but the most well-known was the leading crypto-zoologist, in the USA Dr. Roy Mackal of the University of Chicago. He has made multiple expeditions. In 1981, he spent $250,000 on a 9-week expedition looking for **Mokele-mbembe**.

James Powell, who worked with Dr. Mackal, showed drawings of many different kinds of animals to the natives; some were used particularly to test the honesty of their responses. When shown a giraffe, they admitted that they lived to the north of them. When shown a bear, they responded that they didn't have them at all. When shown the picture of a *Sauropod* dinosaur, they matter-of-factly identified it as **Mokele-mbembe** and waited to be shown the next picture. When shown a *Plesiosaur*, they identified it as **N'yamala**. *Tyrannosaurus, Stegosaurus,* and *Triceratops* were unknown to the natives but they recognized the *Pterodactyl* and called it a bat. [120]

In 1983, biologist Marcellin Agnagna from the Belgian Congo's capital saw the creature in a Congolese lake. He didn't get a photograph because, in the heat of the moment, he forgot to remove the lens cap of his camera; it could happen to the best of us. Upon his return, he did sketch the creature for a class and said, "The animal we saw was **Mokele-mbembe**." [121] The movie *Baby ... Secret of the Lost Legend* was based on sightings of this reptile.

The most recent sighting of a "dinosaur-like reptile" known at the time of this printing was reported in Papua New Guinea's newspaper *The Independent* on December 30, 1999. Villagers traveling in a canoe reported seeing the creature wading in shallow water near Boboa. The next day, a pastor and a church elder saw the animal not far from the original sighting. The animal is described as having a body "as long as a dump truck." It had a long neck and a long slender tail. It walked on its hind legs, which were described to be "as thick as coconut palm tree trunks," while its forelegs were smaller. Its head was similar to a cow's head with large eyes and "sharp teeth as long as fingers." The skin was described as similar to that of a crocodile, and it had "largish triangular scoops on the back." It sounds like there may still be some dinosaurs hiding in certain remote areas. [122]

Sadly, the post-Flood environment was not as friendly to the huge plants and animals

1983 sketch of Mokele-mbembe drawn by biologist Marcellin Agnagna

as the pre-Flood world had been, as seen by the fossil remains of giant creatures, not just reptilian. After the Flood, dragons, including dinosaurs, evidently did repopulate many areas of the world, as evidenced by the various historical accounts and ancient art that we have explored. Many animals that had thrived during the Ice Age after the Flood, became extinct with the rapid climatic and sea level changes, which adversely affected many previously favorable habitats. (Refer to Appendix B Part 7 for more information in this area.) Dragons and monsters have become increasingly scarce and, in most cases, extinct, because man and large animals, especially huge reptiles, don't live together "happily ever after." As people move in, wildlife moves out or are removed if they are a threat to life or property.

An example is the huge fish that was killed off of Knights Key, Florida, on June 1, 1912. The article accompanying the photograph states that the monster was a deep-sea fish driven to the surface by a volcanic eruption. Captain Thompson and his crew were in his 20-foot boat. They reportedly had a 39-hour fight with the gargantuan fish and used 5 harpoons and 150 bullets to subdue it. It was towed in and exhibited from Florida to Washington DC, where it was eventually displayed at the Hippodrome Building in 1913. The "sea monster" was reported as being a baby of its kind and the only one of its species in existence, although the article doesn't report what species that was. It was 45 feet long, weighed 30,000 pounds, measured 23 feet 9 inches in circumference, and had swallowed a 1500-pound blackfish. It had a 10-foot tail from tip to tip, a dorsal fin that was 3 feet long and 2 feet 9 inches wide, and a liver that weighed 1700 pounds!

This creature was apparently killed and preserved specifically for the purpose of drawing crowds and producing income for Captain Thompson's Aquarium. I suppose that local people would have wanted it removed out of fear that someone might be swallowed in its 43-inch-wide, 38-inch-high mouth.

One way or another, man and large animals do not live in close proximity to one another for very long. Usually it was the animals that were forced to relocate, or they just disappeared completely. Evidently, both scenarios have occurred throughout the history of these marvelous, mysterious, reptilian monsters.

The Jurassic Period

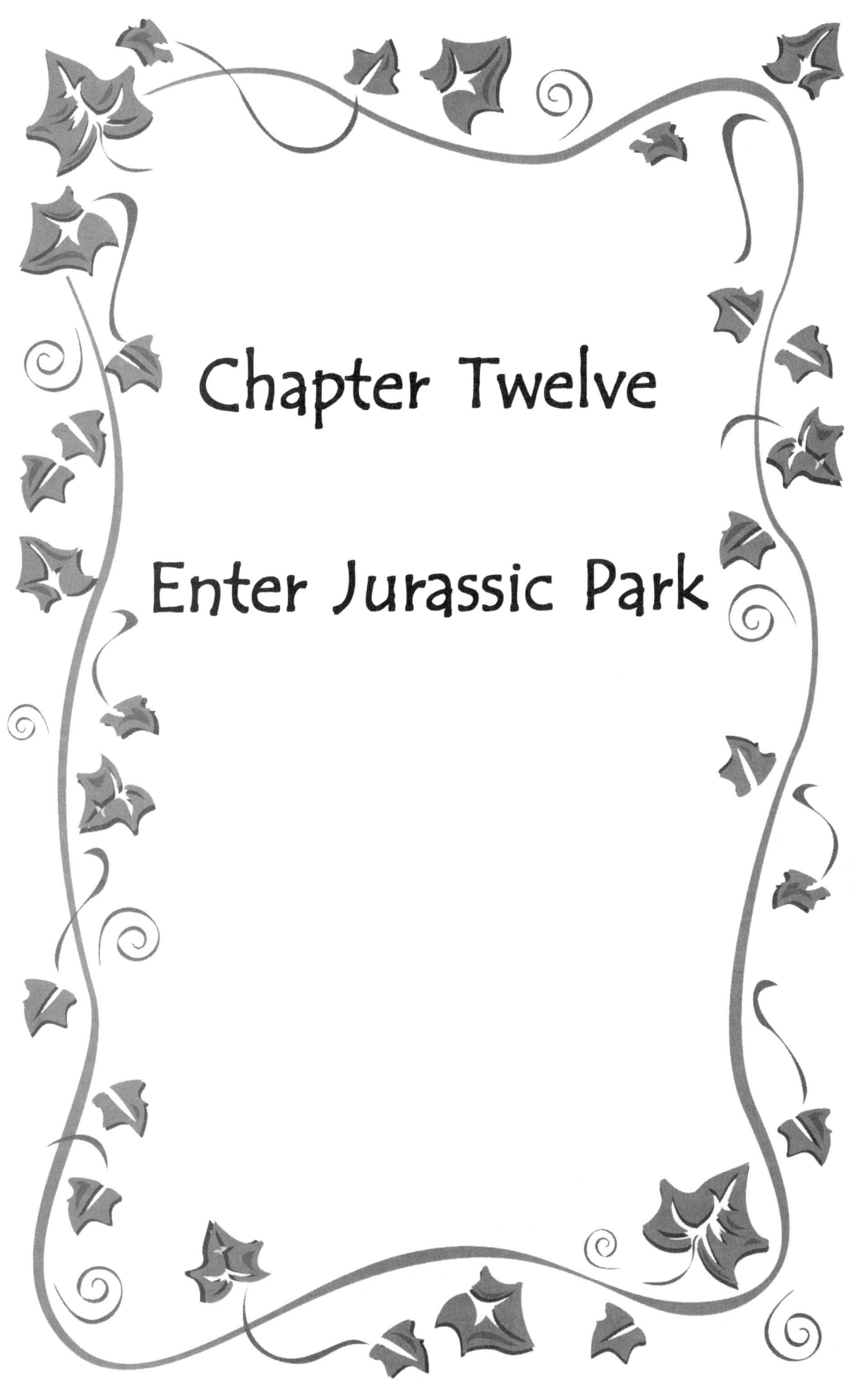

Chapter Twelve

Enter Jurassic Park

Enter Jurassic Park

The Dinosaurs' Demise

The evolutionists teach that dinosaurs lived millions of years ago during the "Mesozoic Period" after evolving up from lower animals. They supposedly ruled the earth during the "Age of the Reptiles," also known as the Jurassic Period, around 100 million years ago. (For a Biblical perspective on these geologic periods, please refer to Appendix C.) Around 65 million years ago during the "Cretaceous Period," something happened to cause the dinosaurs to disappear. There are many theories put forth within the evolutionary camp on what disaster caused the dinosaurs' demise.

One theory suggests that the dinosaurs were just too big to survive, and so they became extinct. When interpreting the fossils, it appears that the large and small dinosaurs all became extinct around the same time. If their gigantic size was a disadvantage causing their extinction, why didn't the smaller dinosaurs survive, as did the smaller turtles and crocodiles?

Some have suggested that disease may have caused a dinosaur epidemic, wiping them out. There is evidence of disease in the fossil record; for example, the *Tyrannosaurus rex* Sue apparently had gout, and others show signs of cancer and other diseases. This is because after Adam's sin, the curse of death had caused all creation to start deteriorating (or devolving), and so disease and death had become the norm. If an epidemic was responsible for the demise of the dinosaurs, the disease would have had to encircle the globe, killing a huge variety of creatures, from *Theropods* and *Sauropods* to *Ceratopsians, Stegosaurians, Ankylosaurs,*

The Fight

Hadrosaurs, not to mention the *Pterosaurs* and marine reptiles. Yet it did not kill all the reptiles. This seems unlikely at best.

The fossil evidence records drastic climate changes in the past. Many believe this could have caused the dinosaurs' extinction because large animals don't do very well in rapidly changing climatic conditions; they don't seem to be as flexible and resilient as some of the smaller creatures. If this is the case, we must once again ask ourselves why the smaller dinosaurs died off at the same time as the larger dinosaurs, yet other reptiles that are considered closely related to the dinosaurs in evolutionary terms, like the crocodile, survived. The rapidly changing climatic conditions did adversely affect specific species that happened to congregate in areas where the habitat became hostile too quickly for them to escape. But dinosaurs were spread throughout the world, and the climatic changes were in particular latitudes as the storm patterns changed. For more information on the Ice Age and rapid climatic changes, please refer to Appendix B Part 7.

One theory suggests that dinosaurs may have been insensitive to the taste of plants, a trait that modern experiments indicate exists in turtles. This theory further suggests that if the dinosaurs were insensitive to the taste of the plants (an assumption), they might have eaten too many poisonous plants and died out. Consequently, as the *Carnosaurs* ate the poisoned herbivores, they were eventually poisoned also. If dinosaurs were poisoned in this way, then why have turtles survived from ancient times to the present with their "lack of taste"?

Maybe the great dinosaur disappearance was due to egg problems. Paleontologists have found *Sauropod* eggs in France that had unusually thin shells. It would be hard for this theory to explain how all the different dinosaur species died out because (1) a small sample of one species of eggs had thin shells and (2) some dinosaurs may have given birth to live young as some reptiles do today.

Maybe mammals ate too many of the dinosaurs' eggs. The evolutionists believe that mammals were just evolving onto the scene when dinosaurs were dying out. It has been suggested that the mammals feasted on dinosaur omelets, and thus dinosaurs disappeared. Mammals still prey on the eggs of reptiles and birds today, and yet a mass extinction hasn't occured in those creatures.

It has been suggested that the mammals caused the dinosaurs' demise by eating too much of the food supply! If so, they might have starved our ravenous reptiles to death. Even in the evolutionary interpretation, this suggestion doesn't fit, because the fossil record shows dinosaurs along with plants in all the different layers. A mammalian assault lasting

 An asteroid hitting the Earth

for extended periods is not supported by current observations of animal behavior, either.

Even the stars are on the suspect list. Maybe a supernova (a large explosion and huge energy surge at the death of a star) occurred that was so powerful, it devastated the earth, causing dramatic climatic changes and killing many different life forms with gamma-ray bombardment. Amazingly, these deadly rays must have been very selective as to what they killed. Since the dinosaurs as well as the ammonites (extinct spiral mollusks) became extinct at the same time, size and location didn't matter in the selection process. Yet the small mammals and the birds (into which the dinosaurs supposedly evolved) survived somehow.

The asteroid theory is currently popular, as seen in movies using this theme, like *Armageddon,* the TV movie *Asteriod,* or even the children's movie *Dinosaurs.* This scenario suggests that one or more huge meteorites, asteroids, or comets slammed into planet earth, tearing the crust of the earth open as it hit. The impact is believed to have caused huge tsunamis to pass all over the planet, drowning almost everything in their path. The crust-tearing impact is also believed to have thrown up ash and aerosols, like those that accompany volcanic eruptions. This would reflect the sun's warmth back into outer space, causing one of many ice ages to start. This ice-age environment, with quickly changing climates and sea levels, made it difficult for the large animals, including the dinosaurs, to survive.

Man isn't believed to have evolved until over 60 million years after dinosaurs became extinct, so man should have never seen dinosaurs. Evolutionists get these ideas from how they interpret the rocks and fossils worldwide. Please notice that any mention of a catastrophe like the world-covering Genesis Flood is obviously absent, when wearing Naturalistic Spectacles.

Translating an Evolutionary Interpretation into a Biblical Interpretation

(*We are destroying speculations and every lofty thing raised up against the knowledge of God, and we are taking every thought captive to the obedience of Christ* - **2 Cor. 10:5**)

Interestingly, when evolutionists read the rocks and fossils of the Geologic Column and the scientific evidence, they can see that God opened the fountains of the deep (credited to asteroid impact), they can see all the animals that died in the great Flood (thus the variety of theories for their demise), and they can even see the post-Flood Ice Age (though evolutionists believe there were many ice ages instead of only one). They misinterpret when it happened because of their old earth perspective; the one Ice Age becomes many and the one Flood becomes many, local catastrophes instead of one cataclysmic event.

Helping Others See through Biblical Spectacles

Once a Christian is aware of how the rocks and fossils can be translated into a Biblical view (found in Appendix C), they are in a position to share the Truth, which will set others free. We can share that we too believe the dinosaurs lived at a time when the earth's environment was very different, the pre-Flood world. We too believe a world-changing event occurred, fracturing the crust of the earth, causing tsunamis and releasing enormous amounts of volcanic destruction, the Genesis Flood. We agree there was possibly one super-continent, which broke into the 7 continents of today; but we believe it happened catastrophically, not slowly. We too believe these events brought on an ice age, which resulted in many radical and rapid climatic and sea level changes, causing the extinctions of many kinds of creatures blessed enough to have made it through the Flood.

We can then share how only the air-breathing land animals that were inside the Ark survived the yearlong cataclysm, and only 8 people out of possible millions survived the Flood. Only those who trusted God and rode out the storm in the God-provided place of safety from the first judgment survived.

Then we can share that there will be a second judgment. The Bible says in 2 Peter 3:10:

But the day of the Lord will come like a thief, in which the heavens will pass away with a roar and the elements will be destroyed with intense heat, and the earth and its works will be burned up.

The next judgment will be by fire, instead of water. The Big Bang was not in the past; it's coming in the future, and it means total destruction for anyone outside God's provided means of passing through the coming judgment. Just as God in His grace provided the Ark for safe passage through the first judgment, God has provided a safe passage through the judgment to come; His name is Yeshua Ha Meshiach, also called Jesus, the Jewish Messiah.

The only safe passage through the coming judgment is through faith in the precious blood of Yeshua, the ultimate Passover lamb, shed on the cross at Calvary to pay the debt of our sin and buy us out of sin's bondage. Yeshua is not just eternal fire insurance. Once we are blessed to know Him as our personal Lord, then life really begins. We no longer have to unsuccessfully attempt to control everything around us, because we can finally let God be God. We have the peace of knowing that He has everything under control. If He could speak the universe into existence, then surely He can handle whatever comes our way.

We have the joy of knowing that He really hears our prayers, He really cares when we hurt and when we obey or disobey. Thankfully, He's always there with arms open wide waiting for us, His wayward children, to repent (through His lovingkindness) and return to Him, washed clean from our sin by His blood. His name is Yeshua or Jesus, the Jewish Messiah, and through Him we are adopted into the family of God's chosen people. What a privilege, what a story; that's why it's called the gospel, which means "good news."

Instead of dinosaurs being a subject that causes God's people intimidation and insecurity, they can now become the missionary lizards God meant for them to be!

Conclusion

In conclusion thier are two main types of belief systems in the world today. Those who wear Naturalistic Spectacles believe that dinosaurs died off millions of years ago and man never lived among them. Those who wear Biblical Spectacles believe man and dinosaurs were created on the sixth day of creation, 6000 years ago and dinosaurs were around until recently, possibly with some still hiding in remote areas today.

Evolutionists aren't comfortable with the idea that man lived at the same time as dinosaurs, because it undermines the credibility of their belief system. Therefore, evidence that might point to people and dinosaurs cohabitating is ridiculed or explained away as best they can. In the book *The Dragons of Eden*, outspoken evolutionist Professor Carl Sagan, in an attempt to explain the consistency of dragon legends worldwide, said;

   they are fossil memories of the time of

dinosaurs, come down to us through a general memory inherited from the early mammals, our ancestors, who had to compete with the great predatory lizard.[123]

There is no known scientific way to pass on memory by heredity. This is really reaching to explain away a large amount of historical evidence that dinosaurs and man lived alongside one another and were not separated by millions of years of evolution and death.

In 1995 Russian journalist Alexander Bushev reported that more than 3000 giant three-toed dinosaur footprints were found in Turkmenistan, and among them were bare human footprints! Because of his evolutionary belief, he suggested that they were made by an extraterrestrial "who walked in his swimming suit along the sea-side" with the dinosaurs. The evolutionary viewpoint frequently requires that some interesting hypotheses be concocted in order to deal with all the scientific data that don't really fit the Evolutionary Model of Origins.[124] Maybe they needed to take off their Naturalistic Spectacles. I'll be happy to lend them ours!

In 1990 at Montana State University, unfossilized *T. rex* red blood cells were found while looking at a microscopic sample taken from a well-preserved long bone from a *T. rex*! Because red blood cells couldn't possibly still exist after 65 million years, famous paleontologist Jack Horner suggested that they try to prove they are not *T. rex* red blood cells, because the scientific evidence didn't fit the evolutionary belief.

Tests have been run and evidence shows that hemoglobin really still exists in this dinosaur bone. Tissue and liquids extracted from the dinosaur remains were reddish brown, the color of hemoglobin. Chemical signature tests using certain wavelengths of laser light confirmed the existence of heme units, which are contained in hemoglobin. Extracts from the dinosaur specimen reacted in magnetic field tests in the same way that modern heme units react.

To be sure that the sample was not contaminated with bacterial heme units, minute amounts of the dinosaur hemoglobin were injected into rats to see if it caused them to form antibodies against the sample. If bacterial heme units contaminated it, the rats would not produce antibodies. But the rats did mount an immune response and produce antibodies.[125] So it still appears that they have really found *T. rex* red blood cells. They are painfully aware that red blood cells won't last for millions of years, so they believe this *T. rex* fossil couldn't possibly be millions of years old. But everyone knows that dinosaurs died off millions of years ago . . . OR DID THEY?!

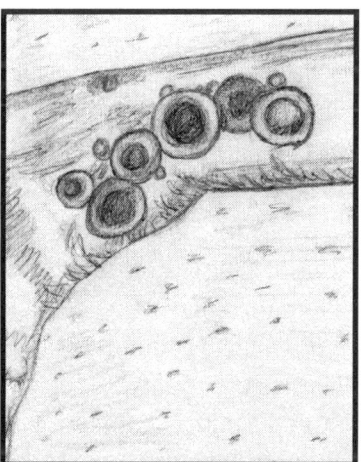

Drawing of a photomicrograph of what appears to be *T. rex* red blood cells inside a blood vessel

Appendix

Appendix A
Biblical Creationism versus Naturalism

Biblical Creationism

Viewing and interpreting facts through Biblical Spectacles produces the view called Biblical Creationism, first described by Dr. Henry Morris, founder of the Institute for Creation Research. The first chapter of Genesis records God's creation in six literal days about 6000 years ago, as calculated by Bishop Ussher in the 17th century based on Biblical Chronologies. The rocks and fossils can be validly interpreted as "young" and "of catastrophic origin" when viewed through Biblical Spectacles: 'young' if one takes the Genesis Creation account at literal face value, and "of catastrophic origin" because the Genesis Flood was a cataclysmic event, which made drastic geologic changes in a very short period of time. This is a valid scientific interpretation, even though it is not widely known or publicized.

In Genesis 1:31, God calls His Creation "very good." From this we believe that God created a perfect world where no death or corruption existed until after man's sin (Romans 5:12). Then the curse of death was put on all Creation (Genesis 3); literally everything in the universe began to wear out (Psalm 102:26). The Creation is under the curse. Everything is going downhill, wearing out (Hebrews 1:11), becoming more disorganized, and going toward a state of lower available energy (many of us over 35 can relate). Rather than uphill "evolution," the Bible teaches downhill "devolution."

Universal decay can be illustrated by the following examples. The earth is spinning at approximately 1000 mph at the equator, and it is slowing down. The sun is shrinking by 5 feet per hour (don't worry; it's big enough to last us quite a while). The moon is moving away from earth at 2 inches per year. In living systems, mutation is a loss of existing information, not a gain of a new trait or "kind" of organism. The entire creation is in a state of dying. The whole system is groaning to be restored to its original perfect condition (Romans 8:21).

Another scientific truth revealed in the first chapter of Genesis (verses 12, 21, & 24) is that living things reproduce only "after their kind." The Biblical "kind" is not the same as Linnaeus' "species" (Carl Linnaeus developed the presently used system to classify living things into Kingdom, Phylum, Class, Order, Family, Genus, Species). This idea of variation only within kind should not be confused with the idea of the immutability of species (the idea that species haven't changed in the last 6000 years and exist in the same form today as they did when God first created them). We see an abundance of variations in God's created "kind," sometimes called speciation.

Within the dog kind, variation includes pint-size Chihuahuas, hulking St. Bernards, pony-size Great Danes, cunning wolves, devious hyenas, sly jackals, and furry foxes. Variations within the horse kind stretch from the sleek domestic breeds, sturdy mustangs, and long-eared donkeys to uniquely striped zebras. Didn't you ever wonder why your sweet knee-rubbing house cat thinks he's a cunning cougar when he's out in the grass stalking an

unsuspecting lizard? Were you ever intrigued by treacherous tigers or lethal lions acting like house cats when they are grooming themselves or playing with their fellow felines? We believe the similarities of all cat-like species are still apparent because they originally came from the group of cats that God created on the 6th day, 6000 years ago.

As groups of animals migrated apart after the Flood, they eventually became isolated from one another. Genetic traits were lost through mutation, resulting in an inability to interbreed. However, recently some "interspecies within kind" crosses have produced some interesting offspring. A tiger was crossed with a lion, producing a tigon or a liger. A llama was crossed with a camel producing a cama or llamel. For the more marine-minded, a pseudo-killer whale was crossed with a dolphin producing a wholphin.

Some evolutionists think that these interspecies crosses are evidence against creation. They mistakenly think that creationists still believe in the immutability of the species. But contemporary creation scientists know that this is just variation within kind and that Linnaeus' "species" is not the same as God's "kind."

Even though we see "interspecies within kind" crosses which have some pretty interesting offspring, we don't see living things *changing* kind. We don't see examples of dogs whelping kittens, or cows calving manatees, or lizard eggs hatching baby birds. Living things just don't change kind. Their genetic material doesn't allow it.

In summary, Biblical Creationism interprets facts in light of the Bible's revealed truths. Through Biblical Spectacles we see the earth's features as having been catastrophically formed in the relatively recent past; we understand that **"things don't change kind"** and that mutation causes a loss of information, as a result of the curse and devolution.

Naturalism (Evolutionism)

A view of the universe through the Naturalist's Spectacles gives a totally different picture. This view currently includes the beginning of the universe through the sudden appearance of matter, energy, space, and time between 8 and 20 billion years ago. The matter-space-time universe formed all the galaxies and matter (asteroids and other celestial debris) that exists in the universe today. This is commonly called the Big Bang Theory.

After several billion years, huge swirling gas balls started to be drawn together by gravity to form stars. An estimated 5 billion years ago, a molten mass eventually would cool into our very own planet earth as it spun off the sun. After cooling and many environmental changes taking place, the first single-celled life spontaneously formed out of the primordial soup (an evolutionary name for earth's first ocean) about one billion years ago.

Anyone who has ever studied single-celled organisms knows that there is no such thing as a "simple life form." Even an amoeba has enough information in its DNA to fill 1000 volumes of Encyclopedia Britannica; that's not very simple! Some people call this "supposed" first life form "lucky mud": "lucky" because all this was supposed to happen by accidental, random-chance processes. Now that would be pretty lucky! (How would you like to be thought of as an accident of the universe? No wonder the teen suicide rate is so high with our society embracing the idea that we are merely accidents of the universe, good accidents, mind you, but accidents just the same.)

Over millions of years, these single-celled organisms mutated into marine invertebrates (sea animals without backbones), which mutated into marine vertebrates (such as fish). The fish eventually "evolved" into amphibians, which then changed into reptiles. The reptiles adapted to the environment, and when things got tough, they mutated into birds, and on and on through time and up the "evolutionary tree," until ape-like creatures evolved into man about 1-3 million years ago. This scenario has been called hydrogen to humans, microbes to man, or fish to philosophers. My personal favorite is goo to you by way of the zoo.

A simple summary is **evolution teaches that living things change "kind" going uphill, caused by an increase in genetic information due to adaptation and mutation.**

Change-in-kind evolution, or macro-evolution, should not be confused with microevolution, which is "variation within kind," or speciation. This concept is easily explained within the Biblical framework. The idea of microbes to man is totally beyond belief in the 6000-year history given us in a literal interpretation of Genesis. Those people who believe adaptation and mutation could have changed simpler life forms into more complex ones must also believe that it took billions of years for the genetic changes to take place; therefore, the earth must be old . . . billions of years old.

Through Naturalistic Spectacles, the rocks and fossils appear to be millions and billions of years old. They are viewed as having been formed gradually over eons of time. Naturalists believe that the same mild, slow, progressive processes observed today, such as erosion, sediments slowly being deposited by rivers, continents moving at the rate of 10 centimeters per year, are exactly what shaped the earth's surface in the past. This concept that "the present is the key to the past" and geologic changes occurred gradually, not catastrophically, is called "uniformitarianism." Evolutionary interpretation needs this concept to establish its essential geologic foundation. The view of the earth and its life forms changing slowly and gradually is the dominant view that colors beliefs about the entire universe when seen through the Spectacles of the Naturalist.

Now you have a brief summary of the two beliefs used to interpret scientific and historical facts. Please notice that they are diametrically opposed. Biblical Creationism interprets that rocks and fossils are young and of catastrophic origins, whereas Naturalism/Evolution requires an old, gradual geologic interpretation. In biology, Biblical Creationism teaches that living things don't change kind, and mutation causes a loss of genetic information (downhill changes), not a gain of new traits. In contrast, Naturalism/Evolution teaches that living things do change kind by an addition of genetic information through adaptation and mutation (uphill changes).

Biblical Creation teaches that dinosaurs and man lived side by side before and after the Genesis Flood. Naturalism/Evolution teaches that dinosaurs died off around 65 million years ago during the Cretaceous Period. It also suggests that people didn't evolve until around 1-3 million years ago; therefore, man never saw living dinosaurs.

There is not a good way of compromising or blending these two systems. The Evolutionary Model continues to evolve. As scientific data is revealed that does not fit the existing model, it "evolves" to accommodate the

new information. Biblical Creationism changes as far as scientific interpretations are concerned, but the part that is Biblical never changes. It's the same yesterday, today, and forever.

Naturalistic Spectacles are used almost exclusively to view and interpret facts (including the Bible) in most places, including many seminaries and Christian schools and colleges. Many Christians are unaware that a scientifically valid interpretation exists using Biblical Spectacles. They don't realize that contradictions arise when Scripture is viewed through Naturalistic Spectacles, including death entering God's creation before sin. (For more information on this, please refer to Appendix F). To compensate for these apparent contradictions, God's perfect, unchanging Word usually ends up being compromised to fit man's fallible, ever-changing scientific interpretations, which were made through Naturalistic Spectacles in the first place! Not very logical is it?

It is important to realize that both creation and evolution fall outside of the realm of empirical science, which involves models, hypotheses, and theories testable by observation and experimentation. No one saw God speak the universe into existence, nor has anyone ever seen change-in-kind evolution and adaptation/mutation causing an increase in genetic information. Neither event can be experimentally repeated. Creation and Evolution are historical sciences. They must be studied by investigating the effects of past events using observable evidence as clues. It is similar to forensic science; the scientist strives to determine what happened in the past from the pieces of the puzzle time has not destroyed. Strive as they might, they cannot be sure their conclusions are correct. Eyewitness accounts are extremely helpful in determining the truth about the past and assist us in evaluating the empirical evidence.

No eyewitness accounts of the Naturalistic history exist so as with Biblical Creationism, scientists must place their "faith" in the scenario they choose to explain past events. Almost everyone admits that creation is religion. Sadly, most people think that evolution is proven science. However, accepting evolution actually requires faith, which makes it a belief system or religion!

Physicist's Bulletin, May 1980, (not a creationist publication) carried Physicist H.S. Lipson's article "A Physicist's Look at Evolution." On page 138, he confirms that evolution must be accepted by faith when he writes:

> In fact, evolution became in a sense a scientific religion; almost all scientists have accepted it and many are prepared to 'bend' their observations to fit in with it.

G.W. Harper also confirms this in the article "Alternatives to Evolutionism" in *School Science Review,* September 1979. On page 16, he states:

> The conflict between evolutionism and special creationism usually boils down to the conflict between rival metaphysical beliefs, and at least in this respect evolutionism and special creationism are of comparable status.

In *Scientific American*, May 1959, C.D. Darlington of Oxford University wrote on page 60 of his article "Origin of Darwinism:"

> We owe it to [Darwin] that the world was brought to believe in evolution; . .

Here is a theory that released thinking men from the spell of a superstition, one of the most overpowering that has ever enslaved mankind.

Evolution is actually a state supported religion, but to be polite, we will refer to both Biblical Creationism and Naturalistism/Evolution as beliefs. To be technical, God observed the creation of the universe, and He had someone else transcribe His observations in the book of Genesis. This record is not generally accepted as a historical account because many doubt the Bible's credibility.

The sad part is that most people don't realize we are being taught Naturalism and Evolution as if they were scientific facts, even though they're not. When we watch movies, go to museums, or read books about dinosaurs, we are usually presented with the Naturalistic/Evolutionary interpretation. We are being shown the universe through the Naturalist's Spectacles, as if no other viable, logical, scientific view exists. We are so inundated with the Naturalistic perspective of dinosaurs that most Bible-believing individuals have very little, if any, idea how dinosaurs fit into their Bible. They wouldn't have a clue how to explain a Biblical view of the great reptiles to a non-Bible-believing friend or loved one.

Appendix B
The Creation Interpretation of Natural History

Part 1 - The Recent Creation

The Creator God spoke the universe into existence in six real days approximately 6000 years ago. Bishop Ussher, a respected scholar of the 17th century, calculated this date by connecting Nebuchadnezzar in the Bible with Nebuchadnezzar in other historical records, then calculating backward to the creation with the help of Biblical genealogies, giving a date of 4004 B.C.

Some would argue that the Bible doesn't require the creation days to be literal days. In an attempt to make peace between the currently popular belief in an old earth and the Bible, many theologians teach that the creation days were actually long periods of time. They attempt to justify this idea with the fact that the Hebrew word for day, *"yom,"* can mean a literal day or a period of time. But, *yom* accompanied by a number or an ordinal (first, second, third, etc.) always means a ***solar day***. Look at the first chapter of Genesis: verse 5 - *"first day,"* verse 8 - *"second day,"* verse 13 - *"third day,"* verse 19 - *"fourth day,"* verse 23 - *"fifth day,"* verse 31 - *"sixth day,"* and 2:3 - *"seventh day."* So in the Hebrew, the word for day is qualified in each instance, thus indicating a regular day.

God in His grace and wisdom, included the phrase, "and there was evening and there was morning" for each of the six days of creation. This double qualifies yom in the

Hebrew as a regular day, but it also makes it clear to us in any language, the creation days were real days. No matter how hard you try, you just can't get long periods of time out of an "evening and a morning."

Just to be perfectly clear, God was kind enough to define "day" for us right in the chapter. The very first time "day" is mentioned in the Bible is in Genesis 1:5, which says, "And He called the light day, and the darkness He called night. And there was evening and there was morning, one day." If the day, the duration of light, was really a long period of time, then just imagine what the nights were like.

To remove any last little nagging doubts about what the Scripture really teaches, look at Exodus 20:11, a part of the Ten Commandments that God wrote with His own hand. It says, "For in six days the LORD made the heavens and the earth, the sea and all that is in them, and rested on the seventh day; therefore the LORD blessed the Sabbath day and made it holy." God makes it clear in any language that the creation week was a real week of real days. (Though some workweeks feel like millions of years before we rest, they're really not.) For more information on how old-earth theology compromises the gospel, please refer to Appendix F. For a brief handling of the popular Gap Theory, please refer to Appendix G.

So the Bible teaches a young earth and a real creation week. Interestingly, out of the hundreds of ways to date the earth and solar system, called geochronometers, almost a full 90% of them are best interpreted in support of a young earth. In fact, the interpretations support an earth too young for evolution to have occurred and are in agreement with the Bible. The majority of people never hear about evidence for a young earth and solar system, possibly because if people start to believe that the earth is young, they may realize that change-in-kind evolution could not have occurred, which can lead to some very radical thinking, such as believing in Biblical Creationism.

One such geochronometer is the earth's magnetic field, which has been measured since 1835. If it has always deteriorated at its current rate (an assumption frequently used by the Naturalists), just 20,000 years ago, the intensity of the magnetic field would have been strong enough to disrupt the internal structure of the earth from the heat that would have been produced. Using the same assumptions, just 100,000 years ago, the earth's magnetic field would have been comparable to that of a neutron star; nothing could have lived here! More information on this and other geochronometers can be found in Dr. John Morris' book *The Young Earth*. Also refer to the website of the Institute for Creation Research at www.icr.org; go to "Publications" and then to "Impact" articles. Media Angels' Creation Unit Studies are also a good resource of scientific evidence for a young earth at www.MediaAngels.com.

Part 2 - The Creation Week and the Fall

Genesis 1:1 tells us, *"In the beginning God created the heavens and the earth."* Scientifically, we know that the universe exists as a time, space, and matter continuum; it consists of all time, all space, and all matter. These 3 parts are in Genesis 1:1:

time: *"In the beginning"*

space: *"God created the heavens"*

matter: *"and the earth"*.

Please notice that God created the universe as a trinity of time, space, and matter. Interestingly, each of these 3 parts exists as a trinity: time is past, present, and future; space is width, depth, and height; and matter exists as a trinity, but it is too complicated to explain here. So God created the universe in a trinity of trinities.

In the second verse, we see that *"the earth was formless and void and darkness was on the surface of the deep and the Spirit of God moved over the surface of the waters."* Matter had not yet been energized, so it was still formless and void; yet, it was perfect for its infant state. The Spirit "moved"; the original Hebrew can also be translated "hovered," "trembled," or "vibrated" over the surface of the deep. Many believe this is referring to God energizing His system. Activation of atomic and gravitational forces would have given the elements of God's new creation their characteristic properties, making the creation no longer formless or void.

In the third verse, we read that God created light, which covers the electromagnetic spectrum. This includes visible light, as well as a wide variety of energy that we can't see, such as x-rays, gamma rays, radio waves, and microwaves.

In the first three verses of the Bible, God describes the creation of the space-time-matter universe and energizing His system with atomic, gravitational, and the electromagnetic forces. That was quite a day!

On the second day, God separated the waters above, from the waters below. We know that at the very least, this is when the atmosphere and the seas were separated. There is a Creation Science theory that a vapor canopy was formed at this time, but it is strictly a scientific theory, controversial even in creation circles, and not essential to our adventure.

In Genesis 1:9, we read, *"Then God said, 'Let the waters below the heavens be gathered into one place, and let the dry land appear;' and it was so."* You probably have heard the idea that the seven continents of today were originally one big super-continent. The Bible seems to allow for this idea. If the water was gathered into one place, then the land could have been in the other place. Also on the third day, God created all the variety and exquisite beauty of plant life in a mature state, fruit trees with fruit already on them.

On the fourth day, God formed all the heavenly lights: the sun, moon, stars, comets, meteors, asteroids, etc. The Big Bang Theory teaches that the stars and sun existed long before the earth, the opposite order from the Biblical account. However, some scientists say that they believe every word in the Bible and that the Big Bang Theory fits into Genesis. They say God didn't create the heavenly lights on the fourth day. They just weren't visible from earth until the fourth day, because it took that long for the cosmic dust to settle.

The fourth day was really billions of years after the first day in their interpretation. Remember that a Naturalistic view of the creation week teaches that each overlapping day was billions of years long. Those who currently popularize this idea are not Hebrew scholars, while actual Hebrew scholars say any lengthening of the creation days, or lessening the extent of the global flood, is changing what the original text meant to communicate. (For more information, refer to www.icr.org/pubs/imp/imp-184.htm or go to www.icr and search their publications, specifically Impact Articles, and search for the word *yom*, which is the

Hebrew word for day.)

We can trust the Creator of the universe to express Himself clearly, and He doesn't need 20th century scientists to tell us what He meant to say. Besides, there are many scientific problems with the Big Bang Theory; the biggest problem is that it goes against the order of creation in Scripture. I'm no prophet, but I think the Big Bang Theory will be replaced by a new theory eventually. Then those who made Scripture fit their scientific agenda will have to find a new translation for what God said.

If you are interested in this area of science, you might want to see Dr. Russell Humphrey's book and video called *Starlight and Time*. Both resources should be obtained and devoured; only a small portion of them overlaps. Also, find any publications written by Dr. Danny Faulkner at www.icr.org or in *Creation* magazine or *Creation Technical Journal*, which can be purchased through Answers in Genesis at 1-800-350-3232 or www.AnswersInGenesis.org.

On the fifth day, God formed all the winged creatures and all the marine life. For our discussion, it's important to understand that this is when the flying and marine reptiles were formed, not just the birds and fish that first come to mind.

The sixth day held the formation of all the land animals, including *T. rex*, *Triceratops*, and *Sauropods*. Then God finished with His grand finale: the creation in His own image of Adam and Eve.

To summarize the creation week, in the first three days of the creation week, God made three canvases: Day 1 - the universe, Day 2 - the atmosphere and seas, and Day 3 - the land and plants. During the second three days of the creation week, God filled His canvases: Day 4 – the heavenly lights were hung in the universe, Day 5 – the winged creatures soared through the atmosphere and marine creatures frolicked in the seas, and Day 6 – God sprinkled the plants and filled the land with everything from spiders to Behemoth.

Originally, all creatures were vegetarians. There was no death of anything with the breath of life in it, until man willfully chose to disobey God. Then all creation went under the curse of death. Adam and Eve spiritually died because their sin separated them from God. They also immediately began to die physically. I believe God did the first genetic re-engineering at this time. The ground would now bring forth thorns (apparently an aberrant leaf gene) and thistles. Creatures that originally had some other functions were redesigned to exist in the fallen world: ticks, fleas, mosquitoes, and other parasites. The animals, which are so obviously designed for a carnivorous lifestyle, were also changed during this event; previously they were vegetarians.

Even though the original creation was now defiled and devolving, it was still close enough to its original perfection that things grew much larger and lived much longer than they have since the Flood. People lived an average of 900 years. It's reasonable to assume that dinosaurs also had extended life spans. Many of today's reptiles grow until they die. A 100-year-old alligator can reach over 10 feet in length; so just imagine how big a 900-year-old alligator might have been. Not a pleasant thought, is it? At that size, an alligator might have looked like a dinosaur.

Part 3 - "The Rains Came Down and the Flood Came Up!"

Approximately 1656 years after the creation (as approximated from the genealogies and assuming man sinned not long after the creation), God judged mankind's wickedness by sending a worldwide, catastrophic flood, the Genesis Flood. There are several common questions that should be answered about the Flood.

How did they get all the dinosaurs and other animals into the Ark? The Ark was large enough for 2 representatives of each of the unclean land animals and 7 of each of the clean land animals to fit on board without a problem. It was a minimum of 45x75x450 feet in size which is almost 1.5 million cubic feet of space. To give you an idea of how large that is, over 500 standard-size railroad boxcars could have fit into it. If Noah was greater than average size, his cubit (elbow to finger tips) would have been longer and his Ark could have been even larger.

It's also helpful to remember that there only needed to be representatives of each "kind" of land animal on the Ark, making the numbers of different creatures attending the voyage far less than if representatives of each species were necessary. For example, approximately 600 different species of dinosaurs have been named to date, which translates to approximately 100 dinosaur kinds who needed to be represented on board the Ark. The total number of species of land mammals, birds, reptiles, and amphibians that exist today is around 20,000. Knowing this makes it easier to realize that there were far fewer land creatures on the Ark than most people imagine, and the Ark was large enough to easily accommodate all the "kinds" of land animals, animals that lived in the water wouldn't have needed the ride. (For more information on this subject, refer to www.icr.org/pubs/btg.b/btg-039b.htm or for an in-depth reference obtain *Noah's Ark: A Feasiblity Study* by John Woodmorappe.)

Most people picture all dinosaurs as being gargantuan, but there were many chicken-sized dinosaurs and various sizes up to the earth-shaking monsters. So how did Noah fit the extremely large dinosaurs on the Ark? Dinosaurs started as baby dinosaurs, whether hatched or live-born. If they were like some contemporary reptiles, they would have continued to grow until they died. If dinosaurs had 900-year life spans like many pre-flood people did, they could have grown to enormous sizes. It would be more logical to take young, healthy dinosaurs onboard the Ark. I personally believe that God sent teen-aged dinosaurs on the Ark. They would be the right size, hardy and resilient through the coming trauma, have a longer reproductive life in the post-flood world than a more mature dinosaur, and everyone knows that teenagers hibernate better than any other age group, so they would have made less work!

How did Noah get all the dinosaurs and animals from all the different continents to the Ark? Noah and his family didn't have to go on a safari. God brought the animals to Noah (Genesis 7). If it was one big super-continent, they could have walked, hopped, waddled, slithered, flown, or whatever they needed to do to accomplish the migration. They would have had plenty of time for their journey because building the Ark was believed to have been a lengthy process. When God called the particular animals He wanted for this mission, they would have obeyed. It didn't have to be the exact Kangaroo who started the migration, to board the Ark. It could have been its great

grand-joey. One way or another, it would have been just the right creature for the trip because God chose them.

If all the water in the earth's atmosphere precipitated out today, it would only provide 2 inches worldwide. Where did the water come from to cover the whole planet, including the highest mountains? The water from the Flood is in the oceans. If all the mountains were lowered and the valleys and ocean floors rose so they were all level, we would be under more than 1 and 1/2 miles of water worldwide today. Therefore, the Flood flattened all the mountains by catastrophic erosion and crustal movement so that they were all leveled. The water from the Flood is in the oceans, and the only reason it doesn't cover the entire planet is because God was kind enough to redistribute it (Psalm 104:8-9) pushing the mountains up and the valleys down, so the water would run off into the low areas.

Genesis 7:11 tells us, *"all the fountains of the great deep were broken up and the windows of heaven were opened."* Many creation geologists believe that at this time, the earth was plummeted with comets, asteroids, or huge meteorites. There is evidence of such activity in the rock record worldwide. We really don't know how God did it, but whatever method He chose, the fountains of the deep were broken up and released. We believe the crust of the earth was breached, and under the crushing pressure of the overlying crust, released heated subterranean water, which then shot high into the atmosphere. As the water shot up, it carried eroded rock and soil from the cracks' edges, providing the dust particles for raindrops to form. This addition of hot water warmed the atmosphere and the seas.

As the crust was ripped open, the single landmass broke into the seven continents of today. Rather than drifting as many secular geologists believe, they were catastrophically thrown apart. Some creation geologists believe that they were moving at several feet per second. This would have caused under-ocean earthquakes, which in turn caused tsunamis (sometimes referred to as tidal waves). These devastating waves and pounding rains broke the pre-Flood world into pieces and washed them away in the rising Floodwaters. Eventually seawater was pushed inland, partially due to the movement in the earth's crust. The waters continued to cover everything on earth, outside the Ark, for 150 days (Gen. 7:24). For more information on what the earth might have experienced during the Flood, refer to the exciting Catastrophic Plate Tectonics Model at www.icr.org/research/as/platetectonics.html.

As the rock, sand, and sediments were carried by the ever-rising waters and deposited elsewhere, layer upon layer of what would become rock strata started to form. Imagine someone pouring cement into wet sidewalks, layered one on top of another. Dinosaurs and other creatures that walked across this wet strata would leave their footprints in the rocks, just like walking through wet cement.

Creatures, including dinosaurs that were buried under the newly forming layers of strata, would be turned into fossils, which are only formed in very unique circumstances. Usually dead dinosaurs would rot or be scavenged by other animals. In floods, the plants and creatures are buried very quickly under the incoming sediments. Due to the rapid burial, oxygen is kept out, so the organisms don't rot completely away. Instead, water carries the minerals in and out, replacing living tissue, resulting in a fossil.

The first things to be covered by the influx of water-born sediments would be single-celled organisms and sea creatures, which weren't very agile. They wouldn't be able to get out of the way very quickly. Instead, they would be buried in the first and lowest rock strata. As the water continued to bring in sediments and new layers were laid, fish, *Icthyosaurs* (a marine reptile), leviathans, and other excellent swimmers would get caught. As the waters encroached inland, the swamp dwellers from salamanders to *Sauropods* would have been buried in the sediments. The last general group to be buried would be those who lived inland and could run the fastest, jump the highest and get out of the way the longest . . . the more agile land dinosaurs and *Pterosaurs*!

Because of where something lived, how fast it could get out of the way and the fact that water sorts things, we would expect to find at least some order in the fossils, and we do. We find the agile land dinosaurs and other swift land animals closest to the surface. Lower in the rock layers we find the amphibians, *Sauropods,* and other swamp dwellers; then marine reptiles and other aquatic life is found lower still; and lastly, in the very lowest sedimentary rock layers, we find the marine bottom dwellers and single-celled organisms who weren't very fast. We do see this basic order in the fossil record, although more often than not, there exists more chaos and confusion than order. Nothing less would be expected in such a violent catastrophe.

Part 4 - Rocks and Fossils

The rocks and fossils found worldwide are scientific facts, which have been named the Geologic Column. The Column is easily explained by the global catastrophe of the Genesis Flood when wearing Biblical Spectacles. When we put on the Naturalistic Spectacles, these same rocks and fossils become the best evidence for an old earth and evolution. How can that be true?

A Naturalist sees the rock strata as having been laid down over long, slow periods of time, through gradual processes, which we still see happening today like erosion and water-deposited sediments. If the rocks were laid down gradually, then the top rock strata would be the youngest and the rocks and fossils deeper down in the strata would be progressively older. If this was true and you dug down far enough, you could go back literally billions of years into earth history.

The Naturalist sees the single-celled organisms in what he believes to be the "oldest" rocks and the marine invertebrates in slightly younger rock above the other. Above them in "younger" rock, marine vertebrates are found, and above them, fossils of the swamp dwellers are found. In the uppermost strata or "youngest" rocks are found the land animals. When interpreted through the Naturalistic Spectacles, it appears that in the lowest rock layers, we observe the original single celled life forms evolving over millions of years into marine invertebrates. Higher in the rocks and millions of years later, they evolved into marine vertebrates, and on and on, up the evolutionary tree until the agile land creatures evolved in the most recent times.

If this is all true, then why are there no transition fossils or intermediate life forms found in the fossil record: no half fish - half frog, no half dinosaur - half bird, no half ape - half man? Professor T.L. Moore, one of the most vocal evolutionists, says, "The more one studies paleontology [the fossil record], the more certain one becomes that evolution is based upon faith alone."

Frequently transition fossils or missing links have been reported in the news as the latest find, such as the feathered dinosaur fossil reported in the late 1990's. Eventually, they were shown to be something within "kind," not in-between "kinds," or a hoax as in the case of the feathered dinosaur. The problem is that the average person never sees the retraction! Don't be fooled! No transition fossils exist outside of the minds of man. We know this because the Bible teaches that living things reproduce only after their own "kind."

The rock strata are not dated by some special scientific technique, as so many people think. They are assigned an age by index fossils imbedded in them, not by radiometric dating. Index fossils are found in a particular level of rock strata and none other. Any dinosaur or anything else found in the same strata are dated by the index fossil. Even in radiometric dating, index fossils are used to select the appropriate date from the resulting range of such testing. Index fossils are the key to dating the rocks, and the rocks are the key to dating the earth.

So how are the index fossils dated?! They are dated by when they were supposed to have "evolved"! Evolutionists date the rocks by the index fossil, and then they "prove" evolution by the date of the rock. This whole cycle is dependent upon the Naturalistic interpretation being true in the first place. Even *Encyclopedia Britannica* agrees in "Geology":

> It cannot be denied that from a strictly philosophical standpoint **geologists are here arguing in a circle**. The succession of organisms has been determined by a study of their remains embedded in the rocks. The relative ages of the rocks are determined by the remains of organisms that they contain.

Bioscience, not a creationist publication, questions in the article "Biologists, Help!":

> Are the authorities maintaining on the

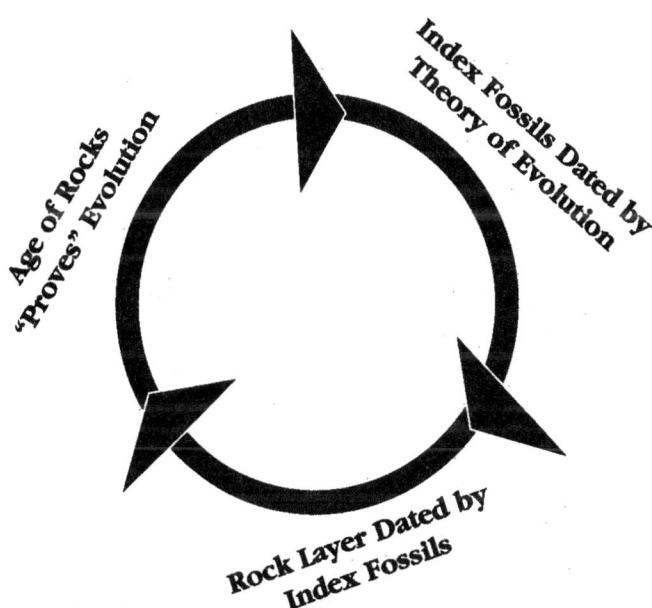

> one hand that evolution is documented by geology and on the other hand that geology is documented by evolution? Isn't this a circular argument?

There are two very different ways to interpret the same scientific facts, the rocks, and the fossils. **Either the Genesis Flood covered the entire planet laying down the rocks and**

fossils catastrophically, the earth is young, and man lived alongside dinosaurs, OR the Flood was a localized catastrophe, the rocks and fossils were laid down over long periods of time, the earth is old, and dinosaurs and man were separated by over 60 million years. Try as people might to believe something in between, scientifically, you can't have it both ways; either the rocks and fossils were laid down catastrophically during the Flood or the rocks and fossils were laid down over long slow periods of time. Those scientists who say they believe the Bible but still hold to an old earth often teach that the Genesis Flood covered "the world as Noah knew it" and was a local Mediterranean phenomenon, not a world-covering event. This is not what Scripture says. Investigate for yourself. Genesis 6-9 is clear that the mountains were covered, and everything that breathed air and didn't swim really well died.

People who believe the earth is old must also believe that dinosaurs and man were separated by millions of years and never lived side-by-side. The Bible as well as eyewitness accounts seem to lead to other possibilities.

Part 5 - Evidence of a World-Covering Flood and Recent Catastrophic Deposition of Rocks and Fossils

There is an abundance of evidence in support of a worldwide flood that inundated all the land, including what are now mountaintops (Gen. 7:20). A layer of sedimentary rock, which is formed when sediments are cemented together, usually underwater, exists worldwide and is around one mile thick in most places. These layers are frequently continental in size. This is the logical result of a world-covering flood.

Marine fossils are found on mountaintops all over the world. Even at the summit of Mt. Everest, the highest elevation in the world, and Mt. McKinley, the tallest mountain in the world, marine fossils have been found. Either all the highest mountains were once submerged underneath the ocean, or they had some awfully talented flying fish in the past! It is important to understand that during the Flood, the oceans weren't as high as Mt. Everest is currently. The mountains were still flattened underneath the oceans and had not yet been pushed up by crustal movement. So Noah and the dinosaurs didn't need oxygen masks to breath because they weren't at high altitudes, even though they really were above Mt. McKinley and Mt. Everest.

Evidence supporting that the mud, which would harden into rocks and fossils, was laid down catastrophically, as seen through the Biblical Spectacles, is also plentiful. Some fossil trees are found stretching through several feet of rock strata; they're called polystrate trees. If the mud that formed the rocks were really laid down slowly, the trees would have had to stand around for millions of years as the strata built up around them. Trees just don't last that long. God does have a sense of humor; about half of these trees are found root-end-up. If the Naturalists were correct, these trees would have stood around up-side-down for millions of years as the mud built up and solidified around them. I don't think so!

Many fossils show evidence of rapid burial. Fish were buried so quickly that they are frequently found fossilized with their prey

still protruding out of their mouths, frozen in stone in the act of catching their dinner. An *Ichthyosaur* (a marine reptile) was buried so quickly that she didn't have time to finish giving birth before she was buried. In the fossil, the infant can be seen half way out of the birth canal with its beak still inside its mother. They were obviously buried quite rapidly.

In 1976, an 85-foot-long baleen whale was found "on his tail" in a diatomaceous earth mine in Lompoc, California. The whale was found in the strata at an almost vertical angle with its tail down and head up. In a normal situation of death and slow burial, scavengers would have taken plenty of bites out of this unfortunate individual. After close observation, there doesn't appear to be any scavenger marks on the fossil, which suggests very rapid burial. It is possible that this whale died due to Flood events and was buried laying horizontally; even in this position, the creature is 25 feet in girth and would show scavenger marks if not buried rapidly. When the mountains were pushed up after the Flood, this big guy was pushed up with it, and voila: we find a whale on its tail!

In 1980 Mt. St. Helens erupted, giving us observable evidence of how rock strata is laid down catastrophically. Twenty-five feet of finely stratified rock layers were observed, measured, and recorded to have been laid down in 3 hours one day, not over millions of years.

A petrified forest is currently forming in Spirit Lake, made from the forest that used to grace Mt. St. Helen's slopes, and the lake water, mineralized by volcanic ash.

Several canyons were even formed very quickly, one of which is called the Little Grand Canyon, a $1/40^{th}$ scale model. This canyon was cut after a landslide caused by the volcanic activity dammed up the Tuttle River. When the river was finally able to breach the landslide, it cut out the canyon, over 100 feet deep of sheer rock in one day. Rock strata, canyons, badlands, and other geologic formations don't take millions of years to form; they take catastrophic conditions. (More information on this can be found in Dr. Steve Austin's *Mt. St. Helen's* video.)

The Naturalistic geologists have compensated for this new information with "neo-catastrophism." Remember, "uniformitarians/gradualists" believe the present is the key to the past, and everything we see around us formed slowly and gradually over long periods of time. The "neo-catastrophists" believe rocks and fossils were laid down catastrophically with long periods of time in between each catastrophe layer. Young earth creationists are "catastrophists" who believe catastrophes in the past like the great Flood and the post-Flood Ice Age are responsible for most of the geologic features that exist today.

Part 6 - The Flood Waters Recede

As the earth's crust finally began to settle from all the changes it had experienced, the waters started to recede by draining off into

Bent Rock Strata of the Canadian Rockies

Courtesy of the Geological Survey of Canada (#GSC 180345)

lower-lying areas. Psalm 104 describes how God caused the Floodwaters to subside into the newly-deepening valleys and ocean basins as the mountains were being pushed upward. Evidence of these events exists in the form of bent and folded rock strata, which can be seen in many mountain ranges. Rocks don't bend very readily; they break and shatter, unless they are bent while they are still in what geologists call a plastic or pliable state. Once they dry thoroughly, they are no longer pliable. These examples of bent rock strata are evidence of the mountains being pushed up from under the Flood, waters; otherwise, they would have shattered and broken like pottery instead of bending and folding like wet clay.

In one *National Geographic* magazine article on dinosaurs, a man is precariously balancing on the side of a mountain in Argentina pointing to three sets of dinosaur footprints that run along the vertical rock face. These dinosaurs evidently walked across the freshly deposited sediments during the early stages of the Flood while the rock was like a wet sidewalk, leaving their footprints in stone. In the later stages of the Flood, the mountains up-warped from underneath the Floodwaters and voilà, the fossil dinosaur footprints seem to belong to extraterrestrial dinosaurs as their fossil footprints move vertically along the mountainside.

Evidence that the Pacific Ocean basin bent downward by 2 full miles can be seen from the existence of hundreds of geyotes (non-volcanic submarine table-topped mountains that used to be islands) which dot the Pacific Ocean Floor. At a two-mile depth, these geyotes are surrounded by extinct coral reefs, and corals don't grow below a 300-foot depth, because they require light to survive.

Part 7 - The Post-Flood Ice Age

Noah, his family, his daughters-in-law, and all those animals, including the dinosaurs, were Ark-mates for over a year! As if that wasn't trying enough, they exited the Ark into the beginning of the Ice Age.

The Ice Age was a time when the glaciers (huge rivers of ice) and ice sheets were in different places than where they are today. Though today the coldest places on earth are the north and south poles, during the Ice Age, you could have gone on an Arctic fishing expedition because the polar ice cap had not yet formed. You could have also gone on a picnic to the beach in Antarctica or on the Artic coast in Siberia! During the Ice Age, some of the coldest places on earth were Canada, Northern France, and Germany. Even as far south as St. Louis would have been under glaciers and looked like the Arctic because near the oceans it was warm, and inland in the upper latitudes it was cold.

The global disruption of the Flood caused the Ice Age; in particular, the opening of the fountains of the deep caused two events that initiated this chilly time. First, hot water from the opening of the fountains of the deep was mixed into the oceans, raising the average water temperature to about 27° C (80° F or like warm bath water). Today, the average temperature of ocean water is 4° C (39° F or like the water that comes out of your refrigerator). When the oceans finally finished cooling approximately 700 years later, the Ice Age would have ended.

Second, opening of the fountains of the deep caused the earth's crust to be breached, releasing unimaginably large amounts of volcanic activity. This spewed ash and aerosols into the atmosphere, which caused the sun's warming rays to be reflected back into outer space (the inverse greenhouse effect), cooling the atmosphere worldwide. Naturalists admit that if all the volcanic activity found in the earth's rock layers occurred in hundreds of years (as it did) instead of their presumed millions, it would have caused a "nuclear winter scenario" (such as the indefinitely long winter that was believed would be an aftereffect of nuclear war) making the atmosphere cold.

The air would have cleared of volcanic ash and aerosols hundreds of years before the water finished cooling down because the majority of the drastic crustal movement was finished in a very short time, maybe even a few months.

When warm water is in contact with cool air, it causes the water to evaporate, then condense, and precipitate. Just think of what your bathroom looks like after you take a very hot shower on a very cold day: it becomes a foggy mess. That's because the hot water is

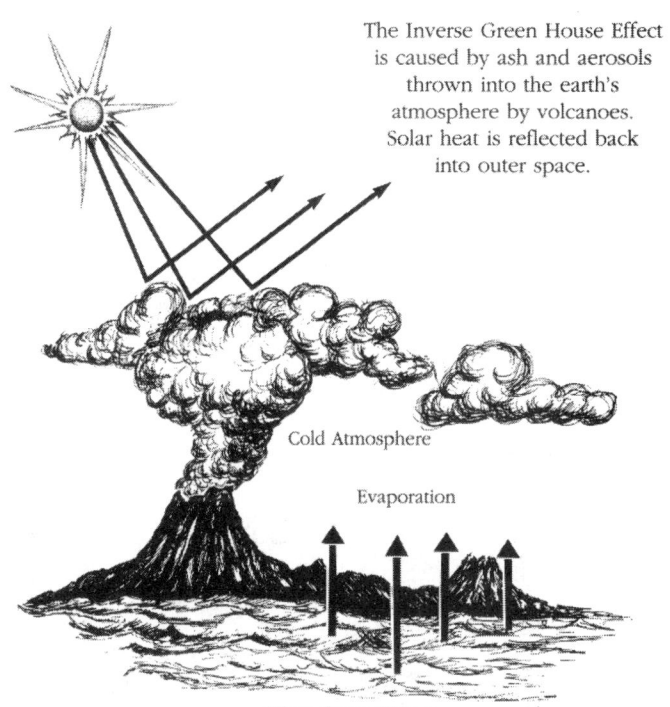

The Inverse Green House Effect is caused by ash and aerosols thrown into the earth's atmosphere by volcanoes. Solar heat is reflected back into outer space.

meeting the cold air, causing it to condense on your bathroom walls and mirror. The Ice Age precipitation would have been heavy and fairly continuous, as long as the water was warm.

A warm ocean worldwide made stormtracks (paths which storms follow), very different than what they are today. In the colder upper latitudes, this inland precipitation would have been snow, which would have started building glaciers. Precipitation in the lower latitudes would have been rain continuous enough to create rain forests in places where they don't exist today, such as Northern Africa (Sahara Desert region) and the Holy Land (and I don't mean the Holy Land Experience in Orlando, Florida). Evidence of these areas previously being well watered is now becoming fairly common knowledge. Creationists, not surprisingly, believe that these rainforests were formed in the more recent past than Naturalists do.

When the dinosaurs and other Ark passengers first entered the post-Flood world, the vegetation had just started growing back, and sea levels worldwide were over 300 feet higher than what they are today. This is because the polar caps and glaciers had not yet formed, and so all that water was still in the oceans. As the water evaporated and snowed inland, building up huge glacial ranges, sea levels would have progressively dropped.

It would have taken an estimated 250 years for the glaciers to be at their largest and most expansive, dropping sea levels over 300 feet below what they are today, exposing the continental shelves. The Bible's description in Genesis 11 of the Division of the Nations, also known as the Tower of Babel, occurred at this time. Mesopotamia's Fertile Crescent was just down the way from the mountains of Ararat where the Ark landed. People, as well as our monster reptiles and other creatures, were able to migrate from the area of the Fertile Crescent into the other five continents presently inhabited by humans by crossing the exposed continental shelves.

Warm oceans caused the climate to be temperate in coastal areas, including England and the coastal regions of Siberia, Alaska, and

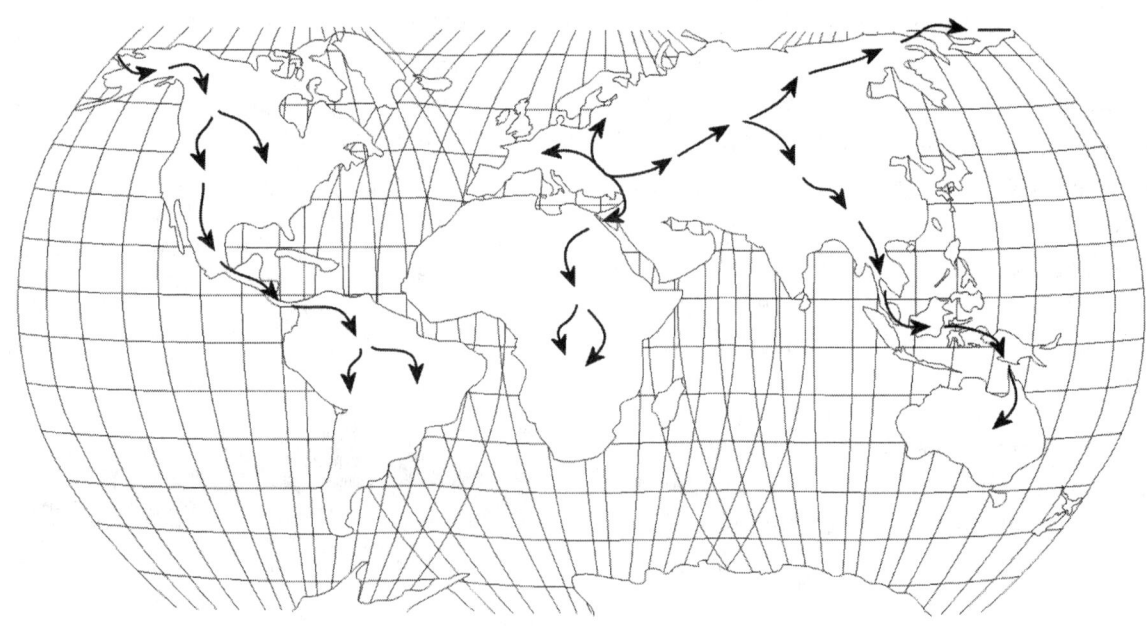

Antarctica. The Arctic Ocean was still ice free, allowing herds of mammoth and other creatures to proliferate in Siberia and Alaska. Evidence of this is found in the Arctic Ocean just off the coast of Siberia. An almost inexhaustible supply of ivory from mammoth tusks is said to exist there.

We believe the Ice Age was an aftereffect of the Flood and ended around 700 years later. These estimates are based upon the time required for the earth's oceans to cool, causing weather patterns to shift rapidly and creating drastic environmental changes.

For example, areas that had received heavy rains during the Ice Age became deserts. The Sahara Desert had been lush and tropical during the post-Flood past. There are lakes with crocodiles in the Sahara surrounded by hundreds of miles of harsh desert, remnants from the Ice Age environment. Dinosaurs, that took up residence in the rain forests of North Africa and inland Australia later found themselves in very arid, inhospitable regions and either migrated or died.

Many of the larger animals became extinct during the late stages of the Ice Age. They didn't adjust as well to sudden environmental changes as their smaller counterparts did. Melting glaciers in middle latitudes caused extreme local flooding. Many animals were caught in bogs and marshes formed by this glacial melt. Mammoths and woolly rhinos had found safety from forbiddingly cold weather for hundreds of years by migrating to the relatively warm coastal areas. But then the oceans cooled, and what used to be a safe retreat to the beach became a frozen death march.

We believe that the Ice Age was caused by the Flood around 2344 B.C. (by Bishop Ussher's reckoning) and ended around 1700 B.C. This would have been about the time Joseph with "the coat of many colors" was in Pharaoh's prison. The drastic shifts in weather patterns accompanying the end of the Ice Age could have caused the seven years of feast and seven years of famine in the Holy Land and Egypt as prophesied in Pharaoh's dream and interpreted through God's grace by Joseph.

As the atmosphere cleared and the air warmed, many inland glaciers started to melt, causing local flooding, laying layers of mud and fossils in certain regions above the Flood strata. As glacial melt waters ran off into the Arctic Ocean, the fresh water would have floated on top of the denser salty seawater. The fresh water started to freeze, and the polar ice cap started to form.

Appendix C
The Geologic Column

Most people are familiar with the Geologic Column, without even knowing what it actually is. We're familiar with it because it's the source of the Geologic Ages that secular scientists and historians use to date things in the past. For example, our dinosaurian friends supposedly ruled the earth during the Jurassic Period and died off during the Cretaceous Period. These are designations in the geologic time scale based on the Geologic Column.

It's very enlightening to understand how these Geologic Ages were derived. The Geologic Column is made up of many layers of rock strata and the fossils they contain.

These rock layers are often found to be uniformly distributed and in the same basic order.

Picture blankets of sediments that were laid down one on top of the other and then hardened into rock. Each blanket covered most, if not all, of the earth before the next one was laid on top of it. These blankets make up a layer almost one mile thick.

The fossils in the Geologic Column are often found in a very ordered sequence, starting with marine invertebrates (bottom dwellers), marine vertebrates (swimmers), amphibians (swamp inhabitants), reptiles, dinosaurs, mammals, and man, moving from the lower to the upper rock layers.

When Naturalistic Spectacles are used to interpret the Geologic Column, the Uniformitarian mindset is used whose motto is "the present is the key to the past." Uniformitarians believe things in nature have always continued as they do today, and everything around us can be explained in terms of present-day processes, with slow and gradual changes.

They believe the mud layers, which would harden into rock strata, were laid down by these present-day processes over millions and billions of years. During these eons, life on earth supposedly evolved. In their opinion, the fossils are a record of the evolutionary process because of the order in which they are found in the rocks. This is a logical assumption if, and only if, you already have faith in evolution.

For over one hundred years, the Naturalists have told us that the Geologic Column and the fossils within it are the best scientific evidence for the Evolutionary Model and the ancient age of the earth.

The names and dates of the Geologic Ages were given to the different rock layers more than 100 years before radiometric dating was developed. Naturalists still consider these assigned geologic dates as more reliable than radiometric dating (Potassium-Argon, Uranium-Lead, et al.). The dates were assigned by the index fossils found in the strata. Index fossils are fossils that are characteristically found only in a specific area in the rock strata (in and between a particular number of blankets). They are believed to have lived at the time the rock layer was laid down. For example, Trilobites (an extinct marine invertebrate) are found only in the lower rock layers and are used as an index fossil.

These index fossils are dated by when the Evolutionists believe they evolved. The rock in which the fossil is found is then given the same age as the index fossil. The age of the rock is then used to support the Evolutionary Model. This is called circular reasoning. The problem is that evolution is assumed to be true in dating the fossil in the first place.

Trilobite

The Creation Interpretation of the Geologic Column

The *Genesis Flood* by Drs. Henry Morris and John Whitcomb is credited for beginning the modern Biblical Creation Science movement. This book is still available and very informative for those who want to dig deep. It proposes that the rock layers and the fossils found in the Geologic Column could be accounted for by the Flood and three processes at work during this catastrophic event: ecologic habitat (where an organism lived), mobility (how fast it moved, if at all), and hydrologic sorting (how water sorted objects by size, weight, and density).

Remember that the Flood began as the crust of the earth burst open to release the fountains of the deep, and the primeval super-continent started to divide. The waters from below and above eroded away the surface of the land. During the beginning stages of the Flood, great amounts of erosion were occurring, washing mountains of sediment down into the ocean. The "blankets" of rock in the Geologic Column were starting to be laid down, one layer after another, very quickly.

One of the best ways for fossilization to occur is by rapid burial due to flooding. As plants and animals were caught under the mountains of water-transported sediments, the conditions were perfect for billions of plants and animals to be fossilized. Marine invertebrates (clams, trilobites, conchs, etc.) that lived on the ocean floor were quickly buried under the incoming blankets of sediment. As the sediments continued to be carried into the oceans, fish and marine vertebrates would have been caught by the huge influx of debris and quickly buried. Their swimming abilities helped them escape burial for a while, but eventually they just couldn't get out of the way fast enough. Some fish were buried so quickly that they were fossilized with their prey still half out of their mouths.

As the sediment-laden waters continued to rise, the swamp creatures that lived near the shore (amphibians, etc.) would have been deluged and buried. Those animals that could run the fastest and jump the highest, and those that lived further inland, would have escaped the rising waters the longest. They would be found in the upper rock layers.

As everything was washed away by the Floodwaters, those plants and animals that weren't buried quickly would have floated around for a time. As things float in water, they tend to be separated by size, weight, and density. This is known as hydrologic sorting. Due to the Flood, we should see the distribution of fossils in the rock layers dependent on where organisms lived (ecologic habitat), on how well they could escape burial (mobility), and on size, weight, and density (hydrologic sorting). That's exactly what we see.

The violence and upheaval of the beginning stages of the Flood are clearly marked in the Geologic Column. Biblical Creation scientists believe that the Great Unconformity is the boundary between the pre-Flood rock layer and Flood-laid sedimentary rock layers. It is seen in the rock strata going first in one direction and then abruptly changing to another. The lower of these two layers is known as the Precambrian Period. Directly above this layer is the rock whose strata go in a different direction; this is called the Cambrian Period. The end of the Flood is not so clearly defined in the rock layers. Most Biblical Creation scientists believe the layers above the Great Unconformity through the top of the Tertiary

Period were developed during the Flood.

The frequent flooding during the Ice Age probably formed the layers above the Flood layers. Ninety-five percent of all mammal fossils were laid down during this time. Marine life that resided in the post-Flood inland seas was probably buried and fossilized during continued drainage and accompanying erosion. This would explain why marine mammal fossils are found high in the rock layers. Naturalists teach that this process took billions of years. We believe that the Flood produced the rock layers catastrophically, and its aftereffects formed the uppermost layers of the Geologic Column in just a few hundred years or less.

Recent studies in sedimentology (the study of sediments and how sedimentary rocks are formed) have shown startling new evidence that the blankets of rock strata in the Geologic Column were not laid down one blanket at a time horizontally as previously thought. New findings indicate that possibly the whole column was laid down in vertical sheets, somewhat like layer upon layer of wallpaper.

As the sediment-laden Floodwaters receded, fast flowing currents rushed towards newly deepening ocean basins. In shallow areas, the currents moved rapidly enough to carry great amounts of sediments. As the currents reached deeper water, the speed of the flow decreased, allowing the sediments to settle out. As the sediments fell out vertically, they separated into many individual blankets of strata of comparable size, weight, and composition (hydrologic sorting), thus forming the rock strata we see today. It is now sedimentary rocks that cover over 75% of the earth's surface.

The implications of this scenario are devastating to evolutionary science because it indicates that fossils found in the rock strata at lower levels are NOT necessarily older than those found near the upper levels. As a matter of fact, they could have been laid down at exactly the same time if they both exist in the same vertical rock layer!

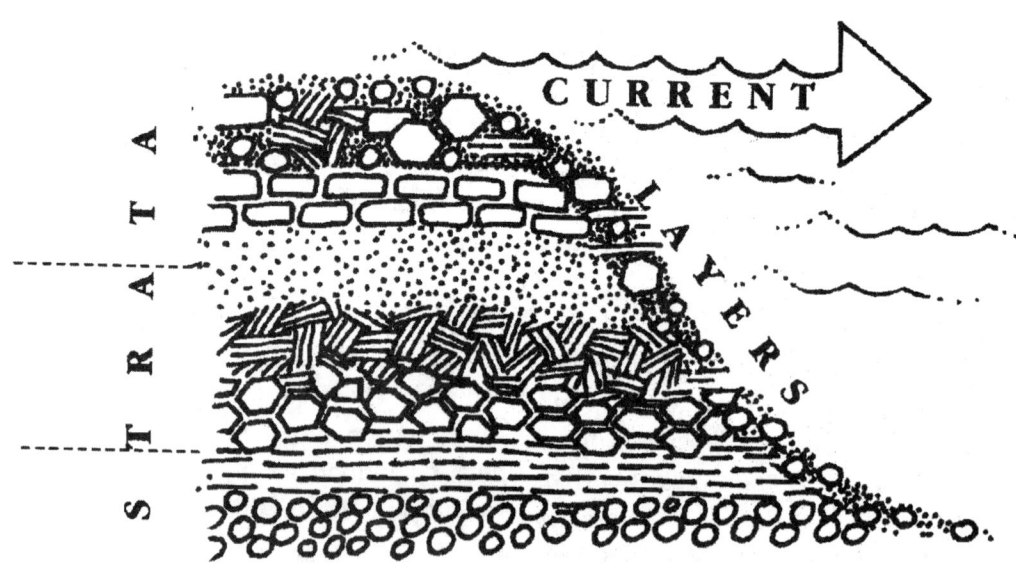

The Comparative Geologic Column

Geologic Column   Evolutionary Interpretation

Fossils Found in Rock Layers	Era	Period	Epoch
Man		Quaternary	Recent
			Pleistocene
	Cenozoic		Pliocene
			Miocene
		Tertiary	Oligocene
			Eocene
			Paleocene

100 million years ago

		Cretaceous	
	Mesozoic	Jurassic	
		Triassic	

400 million years ago

		Permian	
		Pennsylvanian	
		Mississippian	
	Paleozoic	Devonian	
		Silurian	
		Ordovician	
		Cambrian	

1 billion years ago

The Great Unconformity

Proterozoic

          Precambrian

Archaeozoic

Creation Interpretation	**Flood and Ice Age Events Chronology Read from Bottom to Top to Correspond with Column**
Ice Age Ended around 1900-1700 BC **Ice Age**	16. Mammoths and others caught in flooding and rapidly changing environment
	15. Flooding due to glacial melting
	14. Low sea levels due to glacial ice; land bridges exposed and used for human and animal migrations
	13. Volcanic activity slowly subsided
	12. Inland seas receding forming marine mammal fossils
	11. Sea levels very high due to lack of Polar Ice Cap
Noah Exits the Ark **End of The Flood** around 2399 BC	**Warm Oceans/Cold Air**
	10. Major continental shifting completed
	9. Massive erosion of some uplifted areas; i.e., Western U.S. and Grand Canyon
	8. Waters receding, mountains uplifting and Pacific Ocean Basin dropping
	7. Global tidal deposition of rock basically completed
One Catastrophic Year	6. Waters prevailed 150 days
	5. Volcanic activity and the shifting of the continents begin with the breaching of the earth's crust
	4. Global sediment-laden tides deposit layers that will form rocks of Geologic Column
	3. Tsunamis and major erosion
The Flood Begins around 2400 BC	2. Special rain (40 days & nights) Floodgates of heaven opened
	1. Earth's crust breached - Subterranean waters released (Fountains of the Deep)
Pre-Flood	

Appendix D
Evidence of Rapid Fossilization

In March of 1998, very well-preserved fossils of birds, fish, insects, plants, and dinosaurs were found in Liaoning Province of northeastern China in what is called paleo-Pompeii. In the words of paleontologist Larry Martin of the University of Kansas at Lawrence, "It's as if they were frozen in time." The fossils are so well preserved that some paleontologists say they could see an egg in one of the dinosaur's oviducts and the last meal, consisting of mammal, in another's gut.[126]

The Pietraroia limestone, 30 miles north of Naples, Italy, has been known since the 18th century for its well-preserved fossils, including well-preserved fish. One nine-inch-long, privately-owned dinosaur fossil, believed to be a *Theropod*, is so well-preserved that it even includes soft tissue. Portions of the reptile's intestines, colon, liver, muscles, and windpipe were identifiable. The part believed to be the fossil liver is faintly tinted a dark purple; the pigment is believed to have survived. The surface of the gut is so well-preserved that paleontologist Dr. Benton described it as "lumpy and shiny, almost as you would see it after dissecting a modern animal." Small intestine is even present in the anterior (front) half of the abdominal cavity. Yet it supposedly lived 113 million years ago. None of the *Theropod's* teeth had been replaced yet, so it is believed to have been a hatchling. The fossil is presently in the Archeological Administration in Salerno.[127]

Appendix E
Adaptation

Many people do not know how to view the issue of adaptation through Biblical Spectacles. Frequently, in museums and textbooks, narratives describe how nature's adaptations were "designed" for the specific environmental needs of the different animals. First, we must all remember that nature is incapable of designing anything. Nature cannot think, nor ponder environmental needs. We do see tremendous design in nature, but this is strong evidence of a designer. People who believe in the Bible choose to put their faith in the Creator as the designer rather than putting their faith in nature as the designer. Living organisms appear to be designed to be resilient, spectacularly beautiful, and even downright resourceful at times. They seem to carry the trademark of a Master Designer.

Second, organisms cannot express traits that they do not already have encoded in their genetic make-up (genes). Environmental conditions can cause populations of organisms to express specific traits that are already genetically present, but they cannot express traits that they do not already possess in their genes. For example, the peppered moth population in England in the mid-1800's was predominantly light-colored with a very few dark members. The light-colored moths closely matched the color of the tree bark in that area and were well camouflaged, which left the darker moths easy targets for hungry predators.

After 100 years of industrialization and air pollution, the trees in England had a darker soot-colored bark. The light-colored moths became easy prey, and the darker moths were well-camouflaged and survived to reproduce. Due to these changes in environment and with the help of natural predators, the peppered moth population is now predominantly dark-colored with a very few light members.

Evolutionary scientists like to use this as an example of evolutionary change in the peppered moth. Yet, the species started as *Biston betularia* and is still *Biston betularia*. Actually, it is known that both the light and dark variations of the peppered moth lived in England before the 1800's. There is no example of change-in-kind evolution in this situation.

This popular evolutionary story has other scientific problems. The specimens that were used to show the birds eating them off the trees were actually placed on the trees by the researchers. In one case, dead moths were glued to the tree by University of Massachusetts biologist Theodore Sargent for a NOVA documentary. Jerry Coyne, evolutionary biologist of the University of Chicago, agrees that "the prize horse in [their] stable," the peppered moth story, must be discarded! [128]

Appendix F
Dangers of Old Earth Beliefs within the Church

Most people think that the age of the earth is a scientific issue, not a theological issue, and surely not worth any dissension within the church. Busily serving God and His people, many dedicated servants of our Lord are unaware of the serious nature of this seemingly harmless "side issue." Some Christians hold firmly to old earth beliefs, thinking that their effectiveness to share the gospel with educated individuals and intellectuals will be hampered by a young earth viewpoint because it is so obviously opposed to science, while actually it is only opposed to current secular scientific interpretations, not to science itself. Most never realize that the belief in an old earth undermines ***the integrity of the Scripture, God's character, and the gospel message itself*** because it inherently implies death came before Adam and a flood (if any) was local (not world-wide).

As late as the 19th century, the scientific community firmly believed and taught that the earth was young, and the fossils and rock layers were laid down in the worldwide Genesis Flood. During this time, there was a philosophical move away from religion and the belief in the Bible; but godless ideas couldn't gain credibility due to the lack of support from the scientific community who firmly believed science demonstrated the truth of Scripture, a young earth and a worldwide flood.

The modern scientific move towards evolution (an ancient belief) started in the 18th century with James Hutton, the father of uniformitarian geology. His idea was not widely known or accepted until the publication of lawyer and amateur geologist Charles Lyell's book *Principles of Geology* in 1830. It introduced the scientific community to the idea that fossils could be used to date rock strata and the strata must have been laid down over long periods of time instead of catastrophically during the Genesis Flood. This provided the long ages needed for people to accept the miraculous evolutionary change from "frogs to princes." Theology

student Charles Darwin read Lyell's book while sailing on the *Beagle* in 1832 and was also influenced by the idea of Natural Selection put forth by Thomas Malthus. The old earth interpretation of Lyell coupled with the idea of Natural Selection allowed him to develop the idea of biological evolution, which was published in *Zoonomia* in 1794 by his grandfather, Erasmus Darwin. The scientific community had rejected *Zoonomia* because, without long ages, biological evolution was not believable.

As uniformitarian geology became more popular, many theologians started to find ways to "fit" these geologic ages into the Biblical Creation account. They were changing the Bible to fit man's new scientific interpretation instead of making sure their science fit the Bible. Some of the foremost scientists of that period fought vehemently against the idea of evolution. Among them were Matthew Maury, the pathfinder of the seas, Michael Faraday, the great experimentalist in electricity and magnetism, Louis Pasteur, the father of bacteriology, and William Thompson, also known as Lord Kelvin, an outstanding physicist.

They fought these ideas because the Evolutionary Model was not supported by scientific discoveries. It wasn't then, and it isn't now. The only reason secular scientists cling to the idea of evolution with such a death grip is because it is the only way to get the Creator out of science. As Sir Arthur Keith, author of the Steady State theory admitted, "Evolution is unproved and unprovable. We believe it because the only alternative is special creation which is unthinkable."

The scientific facts continue to proclaim God's existence and His glory just as Romans 1:20 declares. These facts are carefully reinterpreted, if not censored completely. If the Bible is true, then the Creator exists, and so does our sin. And let's face it, our sinfulness is a painful reality. Evolution falsely frees its believers from their sin because if evolution is true, then there is no such thing as sin — a kind of no-fault gospel.

All old earth models are based on the uniformitarian (Naturalistic) interpretation of the rock layers and fossils of the Geologic Column being laid down over eons of time. If the Flood occurred as described in Genesis 6-9, then the only "hard evidence" for an old earth disappears. To compensate for this, many old earth theologies teach that Genesis 6-9 actually describes a local Mediterranean flood, killing all human life but not of global proportions. There is overwhelming scientific evidence supporting the Bible's description of a global Flood and the rapid, catastrophic deposition of rock and fossil layers. Marine fossils are found at the summits of most mountains, including Mt. Everest. Fossil trees that span billions of years of rock layers by old earth reckoning are found root-end-up. Not many trees will last for millions, let alone billions, of years while the rock layers slowly build up around them, especially upside-down. We see "billions of dead things buried in rock layers laid down by water all over the earth," to quote Buddy Davis' song. This was the Flood of judgment. Through the activity of Mt. St. Helens in the 1980's, God gave us observable evidence of how catastrophic events can rapidly produce things like petrified forests, miniature Grand Canyons, and finely stratified rock layers.

The most dangerous inherent problem with an old earth is that it requires death before Adam. There are two basic ways to believe in an old earth and the Bible, although there are some inventive variations. The first way requires the days of the Creation week to have been extended periods of time, as seen in the Day Age Theory, Progressive Creationism, and Theistic Evolutionism. The second requires a gap of time between Genesis 1:1 and 1:2 known as the Gap Theory (discussed in more depth in Appendix G). In either case, there would have been the death of animals and even the extinction of certain kinds, before God formed Adam. That means death would have existed in God's creation before man's sin. Yet the Bible states that "*the wages of sin is death*" (Rom. 6:23) and that there was no death before Adam sinned (Rom. 5:12; I Cor. 15:21).

Some people justify death before Adam by saying the wages of Adam's sin was spiritual death, not physical death. First, notice that the curse is on the earth (same word as ground in Gen. 3:17), and the whole creation suffers under the curse (Rom. 8:20-22 and Heb. 1:11), not just man. I Cor. 15:12-26 speaks about the resurrection of the physical body. Verse 21 states, "*For since by a man came death, by a man also came the resurrection of the dead.*" This verse is speaking of physical death and resurrection, not just spiritual.

If death existed before Adam's sin, then that means struggling, death, and bloodshed always existed and is a "natural" part of God's creation. As the apostle Paul would say, "*May it never be.*" I Cor. 15:26 tells us that death is the final enemy which shall be destroyed. On the sixth day, God called His Creation "*very good.*" If struggling, death, and bloodshed were already in existence, God would not have called the presence of this enemy in His new creation "*very good.*" We are also told in Acts 3:21 that God is going to restore everything, and in Isaiah 11 we get only a glimpse of the peace of that time. It is not a description of the survival of the fittest, but the wolf lying down with the lamb. If there was originally death and bloodshed, it leads us to question, will death and bloodshed be a part of God's restored world?!

Then there is the question we've all either been asked or wondered about ourselves, which goes something like this, "If there really is an Almighty, all powerful God who loves us, then why does He allow (or cause) birth defects and disease, famines and war, death and suffering, etc.?" Now that's a good question, and there is a good Biblical answer found in the first three chapters of Genesis, but only if we can trust them to mean what they say. (If the earth is old and there was death before Adam, the answer falls apart.) It goes something like this. God created a perfect world, with no sin or death of animal or human life, but when man chose to sin, the penalty for his sin was death. This curse of death has affected all of creation, not just humans, and all the bad things that exist are due to living in a world under judgment, a fallen world. But . . . the good news is that there is hope. God sent the Messiah, Yeshua (also called Jesus), a sinless sacrifice to pay the penalty for our sin, in our place, a free gift which cost God a precious price beyond compare. All you have to do is acknowlegde your sin, and accept God's way of cleansing for that sin through faith in the Messiah, Yeshua.

As to the integrity of the Scripture, Genesis is a historical book, and is meant to be read and understood as such. If the Bible does not mean what it says in the first 11 chapters, where else does it not quite mean what it says?! Some Christians are saying that it is God's infallible word, EXCEPT when it doesn't quite fit the contemporary scientific interpretation of data. Please, let's not forget that not so very long ago,

scientists bled people as a cure to get rid of the bad blood, believed in spontaneous generation, and thought washing hands and instruments between patients was ridiculous, to name a few. Yet we are supposed to alter the clear Biblical teaching of a 7-day Creation Week (Exodus 20:11) due to contemporary scientific beliefs. WARNING! DANGER!

As a college student, I did this exact thing, thinking, "If God doesn't mean what He says in Genesis, then maybe He doesn't mean exactly what He says in this other part either." This very costly compromise undermines many people's faith at its very foundation, the foundation of the trustworthy integrity of God's Word. Not only that, but it once again reflects poorly on the character of God, because if God didn't mean what He said, why didn't He just say what He meant in the first place? Either the Bible is God-breathed and written in an understandable, trustworthy manner, or it's not! It either means what it says and is true, or it's not!

Admittedly, in my humble opinion, prophecy is difficult to understand, but historical accounts are just that, history, and they mean what they say. So the idea of an old earth compromises the integrity of the Scripture right at the beginning of the book! And let's not forget that almost every book in the New Testament points back to the Creation account.

I've already mentioned how an old earth reflects poorly on the character of God because, for those who believe in the Creator God, it would mean that God created death and suffering from the start (death before Adam). It also implies He is not a very good communicator (Genesis 1-11 can't be taken as a historical account as intended). A popular old earth belief called Progressive Creation even teaches that He continued to let things become extinct, and then created new kinds as needed, and there were people before Adam, but they didn't have spirits. What a cruel, inefficient picture and not a fitting description of the God of the Bible who refers to death as the final enemy that shall be destroyed (I Cor. 15:26).

The simple gospel message is that man sinned, the wages of sin is death, and God paid the death penalty in our place through His only begotten Son, Jesus Christ our Lord. If death existed before man's sin, then the entire Biblical doctrine of substitution and blood redemption becomes meaningless. I have never seen an old earth theory that I could have conceived from reading Scripture alone. They all hinge upon trying to fit the geologic ages into the Biblical account. As this book has attempted to point out to you, there is no need. There were no eons of time taken to lay down the rock layers and fossils, but a world-covering cataclysmic flood made them. It seems that many Christians never think through the implications and contradictions caused by accepting an old earth. The saddest part of this whole problem is that God's Word is being compromised without His people even realizing they are doing it, when there is no need, and all in the name of science. The majority of the scientific data actually testifies to a young earth, just like the Bible says.

For a more in-depth look at this important issue, some excellent resources are Dr. Henry Morris' *The Genesis Record* and *The Defender's Study Bible,* Drs. Henry and John Morris' *Science and the Scriptures,* a part of *The Modern Creation Trilogy,* and Dr. John Morris' *The Young Earth* and Ken Ham's *The Lie.* Websites providing information on this include www.icr.org and www.AnswersInGenesis.org.

Appendix G
The Gap Theory

There are those who want to say that the days were real days, but the earth is still old because they were taught a common old earth theory called the Gap Theory. It attempts to blend an old earth with a literal interpretation of the Genesis account. This theory teaches that there was a gap of time between Genesis 1:1 and 1:2. During this supposed "gap," the fall of Satan supposedly occurred followed by a catastrophic flood that is never mentioned in the Bible. It continues by teaching that God then re-created everything in 6 real days. Many verses are used to support this theory, but their meanings must be strained out of their context to do this.

For example, in Genesis 1:28, God commands Adam and Eve to *"Be fruitful and multiply, and fill the earth, and subdue it."* In the KJV this is translated to *replenish* the earth, which in today's English would mean to refill as if it had been filled before, therefore leading some to the belief that God re-created everything after "Satan's unmentioned flood." One problem with this is that in the Oxford Dictionary of the 1600's, the word *replenish* meant "to fill," NOT "to *re*fill." Performing a word study on the original Hebrew word reveals that it meant "to fill" as it was translated in contemporary English translations.

Genesis 1:2 says *"And the earth was formless and void, and darkness was over the surface of the deep; and the Spirit of God was moving over the surface of the waters."* The Gap Theory teaches that this is describing the chaos caused by Satan's fall. Their reasoning is that God doesn't create chaos, so something bad must have happened here. God doesn't create chaos, but when viewing the first chapter of Genesis as a historical record of the creation of the universe, it gives a totally different and perfect picture with no chaos involved, explained in Appendix B Part 2.

In Genesis 1:31 we are told, *"God saw all that He had made, and behold, it was very good."* From this statement and the teaching of the whole council of God's Word, we can be sure that at the end of the sixth day, there was no death, and the angels had not yet rebelled. We know there was no death as yet, because the Bible is very clear that death was brought into God's creation as a result of Adam's sin (Roman 5:12). This was not just spiritual death; the curse of death that God pronounced in Genesis 3 was of physical death as well on the whole creation: on the earth (v. 17), the animals (v. 14), the plants (v. 18), and mankind (vv. 16, 17, 19). Therefore the whole universe is constantly degrading, running down, burning out. All Creation groans for God's restoration to its original perfect condition (Romans 8:21-22).

We can be sure that the angelic rebellion didn't occur until after the seventh day, not between Genesis 1:1 and 1:2. Angels are created beings, and God looked upon His completed creation at the end of the sixth day and pronounced it "very good." If one third of the heavenly hosts had been cast out of heaven because of their rebellion and a flood had resulted causing the death of billions of God's creatures as seen in the fossil record, our perfect Creator God would not have looked upon this scene and called it "very good." He's the One who knows when every sparrow falls, Who calls death the final enemy that shall be destroyed (I Cor. 15:26), and Who also went to such extremes as sending Jesus to die in our place to give us victory over death. "Millions of dead things, laid down by rock layers buried by water, all over the earth" (to quote Buddy

Davis, a gospel singer) and a third of the heavenly host in rebellion and cast out of heaven, is not 'very good' even in my imperfect terms, let alone God's. To accept it, you must believe that all the rocks and fossils worldwide were down by a flood NEVER mentioned in Scripture, instead of attributing them to the Genesis Flood, which is referred to extensively both in the Old and New Testaments.

For a more complete handling of young earth evidence and the theological problems with an old earth, including the Gap Theory, please read *The Young Earth* by Dr. John Morris, Ph.D. in Geology and President of the Institute for Creation Research, or go to www.icr.org and search the publication section. The ministry Answers in Genesis also has an extensive article addressing this theory on their website at www.AnswersInGenesis.org. For a more complete discussion of the problems with old earth theology, please refer to Appendix F.

Appendix H
Dinosaur Digs with Creation Expeditions

As of this writing, there is an excellent opportunity to experience God's Creation first-hand and be part of a paleonthological dig! For more information contact Creation Expeditions for available trips.

www.CreationExpeditions.com

E-mail: pderosa@cleanweb.net

Creation Expeditions, Inc. displaying mammoth fossils

Endnotes

1. Wilford, John Noble, "Dinosaurs as They Lived," *The New York Times*, 8/3/01.
2. Wieland, Carl, "The Bigger They are . . .," *Creation Ex Nihilo Magazine*, Volume 18(2), p.52.
3. Morris, John D., "The Paluxy River Tracks," *Impact* #35, (http://www.icr.org/pubs/imp/imp-035.htm), 1976, p.5.
Note – There were some cases of fraud on a few human tracks from this area around the time of the Great Depression. This does not remove the truth of the other fossil tracks still in the riverbed. For more information, please refer to the above website.
4. Auldaney, Jeremy, Paul O. Rosnau, Edwin Back, Norman Davis, "More Human-Like Track Impressions Found With the Tracks of Dinosaurs in theKayenta Formation at Tuba City, Arizona Part II, Phototmicrographic Ichnofossils with Modern Tracks," (http://www.creationresearch.org/crsq/abstracts/sum34_3.html), 1997, pp.1-4 and Doug Sharp, "The Tuba City Dinosaur and Human Tracks," (http://www.rae.org/tuba.html), 1999, pp.1-5.
5. http://www.christiananswers.net/dinosaurs/dinodef.html.
6. Gibbons, Ann, "Theropod in Progress," (http://www.discover.com/cover_story/9801-3.html), January 1998.
7a & b. Taylor, Charles V., "Dinosaurs in the Bible," *Creation Ex Nihilo Technical Journal*, Vol. 7(2), 1993, p.170. (Dr. Charles V. Taylor has B.A.'s in languages, music, and theology, an M.A. in applied linguistics, and a Ph.D. in a central African language. He is a Fellow of the Institute of Linguists, and for eight years served as Coordinator of applied linguists courses in the University of Sydney.)
8. Taylor, p.170.
9. Goertzen, John, "The Bible and Pterosaurs: Archaeological and Linguistic Studies of Jurassic Animals that Lived Recently" (Grand Rapids, MI: An Article for the 1998 Midwestern Evangelical Theological Society Conference at Grand Rapids Baptist Seminary found at http://www.rae.org/pteroets.html, 1998), p.5.
10. Niermann, (D.) Lee, "Dinosaurs and Dragons" *Creation Ex Nihilo Technical Journal*, Vol. 8(1), 1994, p.100.
11. Blumberg, R., *The Truth About Dragons* (New York: Four Winds Press, 1980), p. 42.
12. Blumberg, p.42.
13. Time-Life Books, *The Enchanted World: Dragons* (Alexandria, Virginia: Time-Life Books, 1984), p.57.
14. Niermann, p.100.
15. Time-Life Books, *The Enchanted World: Dragons* p.57.
16. Time-Life Books, *The Enchanted World: Dragons* pp.44-45.
17. Niermann, pp.100-101.
18. Niermann, p.100.
19. Batten, Don, "Crouching Tiger, Hidden Dinosaur?" *Creation ExNihilo Magazine*, Vol. 23 (4), 2001, p.
20. Niermann, pp.98-99.
21. Time-Life Books, *The Enchanted World: Dragons*, p.33.
22. Niermann, p.99.
23. Bill Cooper, "The Early History of Man — Part 4. Living Dinosaurs from Anglo-Saxon and other Early Records," *Creation Ex Nihilo Technical Journal*, Vol. 6(1), 1992, p57.
24. Cooper, p.61.
25. Cooper, pp.62-63.
26. Cooper, pp.63-64.
27. Cooper, p.62.
28. Cooper, pp.60-62.
29. Cooper, p.62.
30. Niermann, p.98.
31. *Encyclopedia of Dinosaurs*, (Lincolnwood, Illinois: Publications International Ltd., 1991), pp.21,33.
32. Cooper, p.54.
33. Cooper, pp.53-54.
34. Niermann, p.96
35. Niermann, p.98.
36. Niermann, p.99.
37. Niermann, p.98.
38. Niermann, pp.96-98.
39. Simpson, J., *British Dragons*, (London: B.T. Batsford Ltd., 1980), p.60.
40. Cooper, p50.
41. Niermann, p.98.
42. Niermann, p.96.
43a,b&c. Niermann, p.98.
44. Cooper, p51.
45. Niermann, p51.
46. Niermann, p.99
47. Niermann, p. 87 and Time-Life Books, *The Enchanted World: Dragons*, p.23.
48. Niermann, p.99.
49. Time-Life Books, *The Enchanted World: Dragons*, p.33.
50. Interview with Colonel Remy van Lierde on Arthur C. Clarke's Mysterious World, Continental Cablevision, Discovery Channel 22, "Dragons, Dinosaurs and Giant Snakes," 8 September 1992.

51. Driver, Rebecca, "Australia's Aborigines . . . Did They see Dinosaurs?," *Creation Ex Nihilo Magazine*, volume 21(1), 1999, p.25.
52. Driver, pp.25-26.
53. Driver, pp.25-26.
54. Driver, p.25.
55. Goertzen, p.2.
56. Goertzen, pp.7-8.
57. Goertzen, p.4.
58. Gertzen, p.2.
59. Time-Life Books, *The Enchanted World: Dragons*, p.32.
60. Niermann, p.98.
61. Niermann, p.98.
62. Time-Life Books, *The Enchanted World: Dragons*, p.23.
63. Goertzen, p.5.
64. Goertzen, p.2.
65. Niermann, p.98.
66. Niermann, p.102.
67. Duane Gish, *Dinosaurs by Design* (Green Forest, AS: Master Books, 1992), p.16.
68. Trevelyan, M., 1909. *Folklore and Folk Stories of Wales* and J. Simpson, 1980. *British Dragons*, B.T. Batsford Ltd, London. Quoted in Cooper, p.65.
69. Mackal, Roy P., *Searching for Hidden Animals – An Inquiry into Zoological* Mysteries (Garden City, NY: Doubleday & Company, Inc., 1980), pp.58-59. Sanderson, Ivan T., *Investigating the Unexplained* (Englewood Cliffs, NJ: Prentice Hall, Inc., 1972), pp. 41-44.
70. Mackal, pp.55-56.
71. Aylesworth, Thomas G., *Science Looks At Mysterious Monsters* (New York: Julian Messner Publishing, 1982), p. 62.
72. Aylesworth, p. 63.
73. Aylesworth, p. 64.
74. Aylesworth, pp. 69-73.
Time-Life Books, *Mysteries of the Unknown, Mysterious Creatures,* (Alexandria, Virginia: Time-Life Books, 1984), pp.26-28.
75. Reader's Digest, *Strange Stories, Amazing Facts,* (Pleasantville, NY: The Reader's Digest Association, Inc., 1988), p.23.
76. Aylesworth, p.73.
Time-Life Books, *Mysterious Creatures,* p.31.
77. Aylesworth, p.74.
78. Aylesworth, p.78.
79. Aylesworth, p.75.
80. Aylesworth, p. 75.
Time-Life Books, *Mysterious Creatures,* p.32.
81. Time-Life Books, *Mysterious Creatures,*p.32.
82. Aylesworth, p.75.
83. Time-Life Books, *Mysterious Creatures,* p.33.
84. Time-Life Books, *Mysterious Creatures,* p.41.
85. Aylesworth, pp. 77-78.
86. Reader's Digest, *Mysteries of the Unexplained* (Pleasantville, NY: The Reader's Digest Association, Inc. 1989), p.142.
87. Taylor, Paul, *The Great Dinosaur Mystery and the Bible* (Green Forest, AS: Master Books, 1987), p.49.
88. Time-Life Books, *Mysterious Creatures,* p.40.
89. Reader's Digest, *Mysteries of the Unexplained*, p.148.
90. Cooper, p51.
Aylesworth, p.86.
91. Reader's Digest, *Mysteries of the Unexplained,* p.141.
92. Reader's Digest, *Mysteries of the Unexplained,* pp.141-142.
93. Reader's Digest, *Mysteries of the Unexplained,* p.142.
94. Time-Life Books, *Mysterious Creatures,* pp.78-81.
95. Aylesworth, pp.112-113.
96. Aylesworth, p.113.
97. Aylesworth, pp.111-112.
98. Cooper, p.51.
99. Cooper, pp.51-52.
100. Aylesworth, p.106.
101. Aylesworth, pp.106-107.
102. Reader's Digest, *Mysteries of the Unexplained,* p.143.
103. Reader's Digest, *Mysteries of the Unexplained,* p.150.
104. Aylesworth, p.103.
Time-Life Books, *Mysterious Creatures,* p.62.
105. Aylesworth, pp. 104-105.
Time-Life Books, *Mysterious Creatures,* pp.62-63.
Reader's Digest, *Mysteries of the Unexplained,* p.146.
106. Aylesworth, pp. 110-111.
107. Reader's Digest, *Mysteries of the Unexplained* (Pleasantville, NY: The Reader's Digest Association, Inc., 1989), pp.145-146.
108. Aylesworth, pp.119-120.
109. Aylesworth, p.107.
110. Aylesworth, pp.107-108.
111. Aylesworth, p.108.
112. Aylesworth, pp.108-109.
113. Aylesworth, p.109.
114. Driver, p.26.
115. Driver, p.27.

116. Aylesworth, pp.114-115.
117. Aylesworth, p.115.
118. Cooper, p.64.
119. Cooper, p.64.
120. Roy P. Mackal, pp.61-78.
121. Time-Life Books, *Mysterious Creatures*, p.96.
122. "A Living Dinosaur?" *Creation Ex Nihilo Magazine*, Vol. 23(1), 2000-2001, p.56.
123. Carl Sagan, *The Dragons of Eden: Speculation of the Evolution of Human Intelligence* (London: Book Club Associates, 1978.)
124. Sergei Golovin, "Human and Dinosaur Footprints in Turkmenistan," *Creation Ex Nihilo Magazine*, Vol. 18(4), 1996, p.52.
125. Carl Weiland, Sensational Dinosaur Blood Report!, *Creation Ex Nihilo Magazine,* vol. 19(4), 1997, pp. 42-43
126. *Cretaceous Pompeii*, (www.discover.com/cpver_story/9801-3.html), p.7.
127. Jeff Poling, *Skippy the Dinosaur* (www.dinosauria.com/jdp/misc/scipionyx.html), p.1.
128. Carl Wieland, *Goodbye Peppered Moth*, (*Creation Ex Nihilo Magazine,* vol. 21(3), 1999), p.56.

Glossary

aberrant	turning away from the truth or deviating from the normal
adaptation	a change in a living thing that helps it better adjust to its environment
Biblical Creationism	accepting Genesis as a literal history, therefore the earth is about 6000 years old, there was no death until after Adam's sin, there was a worldwide catastrophic Flood which laid down the rock strata and fossils, God created the different kinds of organisms, that do not reproduce outside of their own kind.
bludgeon	to beat with a heavy object
catastrophe	geologic changes that are caused by sudden, violent upheavals, rather than slow, gradual changes; terrible calamity
clutch	a nest of eggs
controversy	debate; discussion of a subject in which people of opposing opinions disagree
Cretaceous Period	1. a particular level of rock strata laid down catastrophically by the Genesis Flood or its aftereffects 2. in evolution, the third and latest time period of the Mesozoic Era, which was supposedly marked by the dying out of toothed birds, ammonites, and dinosaurs and the development of early mammals and flowering plants
day-age theory	the belief that the days of Creation were really long periods of time; this belief is usually blended with Progressive Creationism or Theistic Evolutionism
devolution	the tendency of living systems to degenerate or move toward greater simplicity over time (contrasted with evolution, which teaches that an increase in organization occurs, from simple to specialized, over time)
diametric	wholly the opposite of something
diapsid	a skull with two holes, one above the other, at the junction of the eye socket and the temple-bone
dissension	a strong difference of opinion that results in quarreling
empirical	relying on experimental and observational data
fallible	apt to be mistaken or deceived
figurative	not in the original or exact sense or reference
gargantuan	huge in size
inerrant	making no mistakes; infallible; free from errors
inundate	to flood; to overflow or move with water
kind	a created group of plants or animals that are genetically similar because they descend from one created type, therefore they have similar characteristics and were originally able to interbreed
mutation	a copying error in the genetic material (DNA)

naturalism	the belief that the natural world, which can be observed with our five senses, is all that exists, and that nothing exists which is supernatural or spiritual
naturalist	someone who believes in naturalism or interprets their world through that belief system
Old-earth Creationism	the belief that God created the universe and life as described in the Bible with the exception that the earth and the Creation is (billions of years) old
olfactory	pertaining to the sense of smell
optic	pertaining to the sense of vision
organism	any plant, animal, or living thing whose parts function together as a whole to maintain life
palate	roof of the mouth, made of a hard bony forward part and a soft fleshy back part
paleontologist	someone who studies fossils and surmises things about the world at the time that they lived
polystrate	many rock strata
polystrate tree	fossil tree which extends through more than one layer of rock strata
primeval	belonging to the earliest time or the supposed earliest form
primordial	from the earliest time; the beginning or original
Progressive Creationism	creationism the belief that life developed over vast spans of geologic time, therefore requiring the days of Creation to be billions of years in length; as certain organisms became extinct during these geologic ages, God is believed to have intervened and created the next life form in the evolutionary chain, each new creature being a new "mini-creation"
protrude	to stick out
prowess	superior ability or skill
regulate	to control or adjust
speciation	1. variation within God's created kind due to a shuffling of existing genetic information, discussed in detail in Appedix A under Biblical Creationism 2. evolving from one species to another
temporal	near the temple, alongside the forehead
Theistic Evolution	several variations of this belief exsists but in general, it is the belief that evolution occurred, but God was involved in the process
undulate	to move up and down like a wave
unerring	free from error; hitting the mark; consistently accurate
vane (tail vane)	the enlarged flattened fleshy portion at the end of a tail
viable	able to live and grow; able to succeed or be effective

Bibliography

Aylesworth, Thomas G., *Science Looks at Mysterious Monsters*, Julian Messner, New York, New York, 1982.

Baker, Mace, *Dinosaurs*, New Century Books, Redding, California, 1995.

Baker, Mace, *The Real History of Dinosaurs*, New Century Books, Redding, California, 1997.

Bowden, Malcolm, *The Japanese Carcass: A Plesiosaur-Type Mammal! A Review of the Evidence*, www.ourworld.compuserve.com/homepages/bowdenmalcolm/plsfin13.htm

Cooper, Bill, *After the Flood, The Early post-Flood History of Europe*, New Wine Press, West Sussex, England, 1995.

Creation Ex Nihilo Magazine and *Creation ExNihilo Technical Journal*, Answers in Genesis, Acacia Ridge DC, Qld, Australia, multiple volumes and articles.

Cuozzo, Jack, *Buried Alive*, Green Forest, Arkansas, 1998.

Goertzen, John, *The Bible and Pterosaurs, Archaeological and Linguistic Studies of Jurassic Animals that Lived Recently*, Article for 1998 Midwestern Evangelical

Theological Society Conference, Grand Rapids, Michigan.

Hovind, Kent, *Dinosaurs and the Bible (video)*, American Portrait Films, Cleveland, Ohio.

Morris, John D., *The Young Earth*, Creation-Life Publishers, Colorado Springs, Colorado, 1994.

Mysterious Creatures, Mysteries of the Unknown, Time-Life Books, Alexandria, Virginia, 1989.

Mysteries of the Unexplained, Reader's Digest Association, Inc., Pleasantville, New York, 1990

Poling, Jeff, *Skippy the Dinosaur,* www.donosauria.com/jdp/misc/scipionyx.html.

Strange Stories, Amazing Facts, Reader's Digest Association, Inc., Pleasantville, New York, 1980

Taylor, Paul S., *The Great Dinosaur Mystery and the Bible*, Master Books, El Cajon, California, 1987

Information from the following websites (all start with www.):

christiananswers.net/dinosaurs

creationevidence.org

creationresearch.org

dinosaurian.com

discover.com

genesisministries.com

icr.org/pub/imp

rae.org

Index

A

Acrocanthosaurus 37, 50, 60
Adaptation 7, 15, 16, 157, 158, 178, 191
adder 79, 82
Afancs 122
Albertosaurus 37, 48
Allosaurus 37, 50, 98
Amphitere 102, 103
Ankylosaur 5, 38, 52, 58, 59, 91, 93, 149
Apatosaurus 21, 22, 36, 42, 44
Archaeopteryx 23
Archelon 40, 70

B

Basilisk 80, 81, 82
Baugh, Carl 134
Bear Lake Monster 124
Beast of the Storm Spirits 124
Behemoth 76, 162
Beowulf 6, 27, 89, 90, 136
Bessie 126
Biblical Creationism
    7, 13, 14, 16, 155, 156, 157, 158, 159, 160, 194
bird-hipped 41, 52, 56, 58, 61, 63, 66
bombardier beetle 77
Brachiosaurus 36, 42, 44
Brontosaurus 5, 21, 22, 33, 43
Bunyip 98, 129

C

Caddy 114
Camarasaurus 36, 43, 44
Camptosaurus 60
Carnosaurs 5, 37, 45, 48, 50, 75, 150
Ceratosaurus 37, 50
Champ 124, 125
Chessie 126
Cockatrice 79, 80, 81, 82
Coelophysidae 36, 45
Coelurosauria 45
Comprognathus 45
Creation Expeditions 134, 184
Cretaceous period 15, 149, 157, 172, 191

D

Daspletosaurus 37, 48
Deinocheirus 37, 50
Deinonychus 36, 46, 47
DeRosa, Peter 4, 134
diapsid 33, 191
Diplodocus 21, 22, 36, 42, 43, 44
Drac 92, 95
Dromaeosaur 46

E

Edmontosaurs 63
Elasmosaur 40, 70, 135
Eucentrosaurus 38, 53, 54

F

Farlow, Professor James 27
Fiery-flying serpents 42, 77

G

Gap Theory 181
Geologic Column
    7, 151, 165, 172, 173, 174, 175, 178, 180
Grendel 79, 89, 90, 136
Guivre 97

H

Hadrosaurs 5, 39, 62, 63, 64, 66, 67, 150
Hapyxelor 127
Heraldic Dragon 90, 91
Horner 61, 64, 65, 153
Huayangosaurus 57
Hylaeosaurus 38, 59
Hypsilophodon 39, 61

I

Ice Age 7, 75, 86, 98, 135, 145, 150, 151,
    168, 170, 171, 172, 184
Ichthyosaur 33, 40, 71, 72, 167
Igopogo 127
Iguanodon 5, 21, 39, 60, 63

J

Jehovah's Park 1, 2, 5, 9, 73, 75, 85, 98
Jurassic Park 1, 2, 6, 9, 25, 75, 81, 143, 147, 149
Jurassic period 149, 172

K

Kentrosaurus 38, 57
Kongomato 104, 106
Kronosaur 33, 40, 71, 115
Kulta 98

L

Lake Iliamna Monster 126
Lambeosaur 39, 66
Leviathan 76, 77, 95
Lindworm 88, 93
Lizzard-hipped 41

M

Maiasaurus 39, 64
Manipogo 127
Mantel, Dr. Gideon 60
Megalosaurus 5, 20, 37, 50
Melland, Frank 106
Mirreeulla 129
M'koo 129
Mokele-mbembe 143, 144
Monoclonius 38, 53, 55
Morag 121
Morris, Dr. John D.
    155, 160, 174, 182, 184, 187, 195
Moses 79, 101, 102

N

Naitaka 127
Naturalism 7, 13, 16, 155, 156, 157, 159, 192
Neanderthals 135
Necker 121
Nessie 119, 120, 122
Nodosaur 5, 38, 52, 59
N'yamala 144

O

Ogopogo 127
Old Man 114
Olitiau 104
Opthalmosaurus 71
Ornithischia 5, 38, 41, 52, 58, 60, 66
Ornithomimus 36, 46
Ornithopods 5, 52, 60
Ouranosaurus 39, 60
Oviraptor 36, 45, 46
Owen, Sir Richard 20, 31

P

Pachycephalosaurs 39, 61
Paluxy River 31, 187
Parasaurolophus 39, 67
Peloneustes 40, 71
Peppered moth 178, 179 190
Petroglyph 134
Plesiosaur
    33, 40, 70, 71, 75, 114, 115, 120, 129, 136, 144, 195
Pliosaurs 40, 71, 75
Podokesaurus 36, 45, 81
Polacanthus 38, 59
Psittacosaurus 39, 61
Pteranodon 40, 68, 90, 101
Pterosaur
    5, 33, 40, 61, 68, 75, 77, 81, 89, 97, 99,
    101, 102, 103, 104, 134, 150, 165, 187, 195

Q

Quetzalcoatlus 40, 68, 101

R

Rhamphorhynchus 40, 68, 101, 102, 103
Ruben, Professor John 23

S

Sanderson 95, 104, 129, 188
Saurolophus 39, 64, 66
Saurischian 42
Saurischia 45

Sauropod
  5, 21, 22, 36, 42, 43, 44, 75, 76, 86, 98, 133, 136, 143, 144, 149, 150, 162, 165
Seismosaurus 44
Sharov, Professor 68
Shonisaurus 40, 71
Sigurd 92
Skrimsl 122
Slimy Slim 126
Sordes pilosus 68
Spinosaurus 25, 37, 50, 133
Squamata 97
St. George 92, 139
Stegosaurus 38, 56, 57, 58, 92, 144
Struthiomimus 36, 46
Styracosaurus 38, 53
Supersaurus 44

T

T'annin 77, 79
T'annim 79
T-Zum-A 127
Tarbosaurus 37, 48
Tarsque 92, 93
Taylor, Dr. Charles 79, 112, 187, 189, 196
Tertiary Period 175
Theropods 5, 36, 42, 45, 48, 50, 89, 149
Thunderbirds 104
Torosaurus 38, 52, 54
Triceratops 19, 25, 38, 52, 55, 133, 144, 162
Troodon 36, 45
Tsintaosaurus 39, 66
Tuojiangosaurus 57
Tyrannosaurus rex 5, 25, 26, 27, 37, 45, 48, 50, 149, 153, 162

U

Ultrasaurus 44
USO 123

V

Velociraptor 36, 46, 47

W

White River Monster 124, 126
Witmer, Dr. Lawrence Witmer 22
Wuerhosaurus 57
Wyvern 103

Y

Yarru 129